D0055831

Friends from the Beginning

Friends from the Beginning

The Berkeley Village That
Raised Kamala and Me

Stacey Johnson-Batiste

TWELVE

New York   Boston

Twelve
Hachette Book Group
1290 Avenue of the Americas, New York, NY 10104
twelvebooks.com
twitter.com/twelvebooks

First Edition: November 2021

Twelve is an imprint of Grand Central Publishing. The Twelve name and logo are trademarks of Hachette Book Group, Inc.

The publisher is not responsible for websites (or their content) that are not owned by the publisher.

The Hachette Speakers Bureau provides a wide range of authors for speaking events. To find out more, go to www.hachettespeakersbureau.com or call (866) 376-6591.

All photos courtesy of the author.

Library of Congress Cataloging-in-Publication Data has been applied for

ISBN: 9781538707487 (hardcover), 9781538707500 (ebook)

Printed in the United States of America

LSC-C

Printing 1, 2021

To the memory of my father, Robert H. Johnson Jr.,
and that of his dear friend Sherman Williams.
They taught me how to understand and relate to people
and how to think for myself. So much of who I am comes
from their examples.
The love they demonstrated, and the wisdom and
guidance they passed on, will be with me forever.

And to my mother, Doris A. Johnson, my forever
"Yell Leader." Without your brilliant mind and shining
example of perseverance, this book would never
have been possible.

Contents

"*The greatness of a community is most accurately measured by the compassionate actions of its members.*"

—Coretta Scott King

"*We'll make sure their story be told.*"

—Kamala Harris

Friends from the Beginning

Passion & Purpose

The Reflecting Pool

The Presidential Inaugural Committee is honored to announce the inauguration of Joseph R. Biden, Jr. as President of the United States of America, and Kamala Devi Harris as Vice President of the United States of America on Wednesday, the Twentieth of January, Two Thousand and Twenty-One.

I turned the invitation over in my hand, reread it, then read it a third time, awestruck. I gazed a few seconds longer at the embossed bright-gold presidential seal at the top of the invitation. It was official.

My heartbeat sped up as years of memories flashed through my mind, too quickly for me to even register any of them. My very first friend had made it to the second-highest office of this land. Almost light-headed, I slowly handed the invitation to my son, Patrick, then let out a big smile and shook my head.

Patrick's eyes got big as he held the envelope in one hand and the invitation in the other. "It's not every day you receive mail with the presidential seal on it, Mom! This is…really cool," he said, the awe in his voice matching what I felt.

The gravity of the occasion started sinking in immediately. Until this moment we hadn't been sure if I would be attending. The last time I had spoken with Kamala, in November, she had told me she wanted me to be there. But her sister, Maya, had been in touch more recently, explaining that though it was still a possibility, the number of attendees was going to be kept to an absolute minimum. I had tempered my expectations, appreciating the necessity of a limited guest list as the pandemic raged on.

I had been given some indication that I might still be able to go, but it was only upon receiving the actual invitation that it felt real. Soon my shock evolved into exhilaration— an emotion that had not come naturally for some time. Though Kamala being selected as Biden's running mate, and of course their election victory, had been thrilling, that news had been delivered in the same way everything else had for nearly a year: from a distance, intangibly, through screens, on the radio, over ecstatic phone calls. This was different. Something about the physical evidence of the invitation symbolized and brought home the possibility that the tumult and darkness of 2020 (and the three years before that, to be honest) were nearing their end. In that moment, the luminescent, sloping script on the invitation before me represented the bright light of change we'd all been waiting for, praying for, desperate to see.

———

Over the subsequent few days I started receiving emails from the Presidential Inaugural Committee (PIC) regarding travel arrangements, hotel accommodations, and COVID-19 protocol guidelines. I would be leaving in mid-January and had to keep myself in strict quarantine for seven days prior to departure, then get back-to-back tests with 24-hour results in order to have two negative tests confirmed within the three days before I traveled to DC. I reread the strict instructions several times to make sure I didn't miss anything. I knew this was a once-in-a-lifetime, historic opportunity—I had to get every detail right.

January 16 finally arrived. My heart was filled with anticipation as my son drove me to the airport for the specially chartered flight, which would depart LAX and make a stop in Oakland to pick up other friends and family of Kamala, soon to be Madam Vice President (!), then fly off to DC. Once at the airport, I eagerly boarded the plane and found my seat. *Welcome Aboard the Inaugural Express* read the seat placeholders, with our respective names written beneath.

Shortly after I took my seat, an announcement came from

the cockpit, letting us know that an all-female flight crew had been requested by the vice president elect. I had never flown on a plane in which the captain, first officer, and entire crew were exclusively women! I laughed aloud with delight and settled in, knowing this was one of the many firsts I'd be experiencing and witnessing over the next few days.

A small group of us were departing from Los Angeles, including a few members of the PIC committee; Kamala's best friend Chrisette and her family (which includes Kamala's godchildren); Doug's son, Cole—Kamala's beloved stepson—and also Cole's mom, Kerstin, who has a legitimately wonderful relationship with Kamala. I smiled at everybody but tried to maintain a relaxed demeanor, though I'm sure anybody who looked at my eyes would have been able to see that I was practically bursting with excitement.

I couldn't wait to find out whom we'd be picking up in Oakland! Patrick had kept asking if I had called Derreck Johnson, a good friend from childhood, to see if he was going. Derreck and I had attended St. Joseph's Catholic Elementary School together and have remained friends ever since first grade. Derreck and Kamala met during our senior year of high school, when she moved back home from Montreal. They hit it off immediately (as she did with almost all my friends). The two of them had maintained a close, separate friendship, and he had always been there to support her throughout her campaigns. I was sure he would be on the plane, but I didn't want to be the person calling him, in the unlikely but awkward event that he wasn't going. I figured he hadn't been in touch for the same reason.

After the short flight up from LA, we touched down to pick up the Bay Area crew, and sure enough, Derreck boarded the plane along with a handful of other longtime family friends with whom Kamala and I had grown up. It was a good thing I had a seat belt on, as my instinct was to run to the front of the plane to greet them. Unfortunately, due to the COVID guidelines that had been laid out so very clearly, I wasn't able to do that, so I refrained and instead stayed toward the back half of the plane in the designated SoCal section, waving enthusiastically at each person who boarded.

Once everyone from Oakland was on the plane, I couldn't help myself. I eased my way toward the front to at least say a quick, enthusiastic, relatively distant "Hi!" to Sharon Shelton McGaffie and Judy Shelton Robinson, daughters of Mrs. Regina Shelton, a crucial pillar of my and Kamala's upbringing. I greeted Kamala's longtime friend Gloria Rhynes, a former judge I had gotten to know at Kamala and Doug's wedding. I was thrilled to see Cynthia Bagby and other family members of her uncle Aubrey LaBrie (yet another important figure for us and our families from our childhood). Each deeply recognizable face turned up my emotional excitement that much more; it felt like a mini reunion with people and families I've known for as far back as my memory goes.

On my way back to my seat, given that we had both been cleared to fly, Derreck and I just couldn't help but give each other a quick, strong hug, laughing with almost childlike giddiness and joy about seeing each other. As I scanned the plane, everybody looked that way: filled with pure exuberance and delight. We were all *ready* to go share this adventure with Kamala!

Upon our arrival in DC, we were greeted warmly by members of the PIC and shuttled to our hotel, then ushered along a corridor to go take another COVID-19 test. We would be tested every day while we were in DC, up to and including the day of departure, January 21. Much as when we prepared for flying, protocol dictated that we arrive four days before the inauguration in order to show two negative results before January 20, the day of the inauguration.

The logistics were organized flawlessly. Shortly after our tests, we were given boxed dinners and our room keys. In each hotel room was a welcome gift: a large canvas tote bag bearing the presidential seal and the number 46 printed below it.

Forty-six. Thank God.

I ran my finger over it, still amazed at where I was and even more so at the *reason* I was there. The tote bag contained hand warmers to help us stay comfortable in the crisp January weather as well as all kinds of inaugural "swag," including a baseball cap, wineglasses, and a travel blanket—each item bearing the presidential emblem. Obviously a lot of preparation had been put into making this a memorable experience for the guests. Though I knew it would have been organized by her staff, to be welcomed by these extra gifts struck me as a very characteristic, fitting gesture; it's in Kamala's nature to find ways to create special memories and ensure that experiences are celebratory for those she loves. She has always had that instinct and exhibited it in all kinds of scenarios— whether she was hosting a simple Mother's Day brunch at her home or helping orchestrate little touches for an occasion as formal and singular as her being inaugurated as our first female vice president.

Each evening, we received an email with instructions for the following day, which told us our breakfast and dinner schedules as well as our times to get tested. We were asked to lie low in our hotel rooms for the next few days, to avoid the risk of exposure. None of us minded. It was such a privilege to be there.

On January 19, the day before the ceremony, Kamala carved out several hours for her and Doug to come by the hotel and meet with each family member (blood or otherwise) she had invited. I went to see them along with Derreck, his cousin Sabrina, and Gloria Rhynes.

Wearing face masks and maintaining six feet of distance did not put a damper on our visit with them or make it feel overly formal. As soon as Kamala and I looked at each other, our beaming smiles shone through our eyes and naturally cascaded into laughter—our go-to language for communicating the love and understanding that we share, a connection that requires no words. Each of us had the opportunity to chat with Kamala and Doug personally, take a few selfies with them smiling behind us, and enjoy this special, private time together before the big event. She didn't do a lot of talking and instead seemed much more interested in what each of us had to say. We all remained masked, but I noticed how intently she focused on each of us, making solid eye contact throughout.

She did manage to ask about my two kids, and I shared that my daughter, Lauren, was pregnant with her second child, due in March. I also told her about my nephew, Commander Victor Glover, an astronaut living on the International Space Station. He had asked whether it would be possible to have a Zoom call with her at some point. She loved the idea. I could tell she was smiling as she turned and gestured to one of the Secret Service members on her team, who came over to us.

"This is one of my oldest friends, Stacey." We said hello, and she told him that she really wanted to make sure she got it coordinated to be in touch with my nephew. She later made it happen—they chatted while he was in space!

It was time to say goodbye for the moment. As our meeting came to a close, I lifted up my arms with my palms toward her and Doug, told her how proud I was of her, and let her know that I was praying that the Holy Spirit and the spirits of our ancestors would keep her safe. In response she clasped her hands in front of her heart, expressing love through her bright, attentive eyes.

That night, the eve of the inauguration, I was so excited I didn't think I was going to be able to sleep. I couldn't even lie down, so I laid everything out for the next day: brown tweed suit, black turtleneck, tights, hand warmers, black velvet gloves, black faux fur earmuffs. I wanted to look professional while being sure I was warm enough to enjoy the whole day.

The next morning, we completed our COVID tests by 8:00 a.m. and met in a specified ballroom on the lobby level by 8:30 a.m. for metal detector screening. As I gazed around at Kamala's chosen family congregated in that ballroom, even though we had masks on, I could see that everyone's eyes were shining, full of vibrant anticipation. Colleagues of mine back in California had expressed genuine concern about my going, given the terrifying insurrection that had occurred just two weeks prior. I appreciated why they would be worried but told them that there was no way I was not going to be there for Kamala. I could sense that everybody in that room felt precisely the same way. The energy was one of positivity, pride, and overwhelming excitement.

I kept surveying the crew, marveling at how many of them

I've known since Kamala and I were little girls. Of course, her beloved sister Maya was there, along with her husband, their daughter Meena and her husband, and their two adorable daughters. Derreck, Judy and Sharon, Cynthia and other members of the LaBrie family—these were connections nearly half a century old. It was such a profound testament to Kamala's loyalty and to the value she places on friendships that most of us had known her for decades.

We had each been with Kamala at various moments in her journey to this day. We were visibly proud to be there supporting her. Nothing and no one could put a damper on such enthusiasm and loyalty—not the fear of COVID, not the shocking violence that had taken place in the Capitol, nothing. In that moment, and in many that were soon to come, I felt infused with awe to have such a profound connection with her and our hometown community.

A staffer came and announced that it was time to proceed to the shuttle buses. That was the first time I had been outside in the daylight since our arrival in DC. It had been dark when we landed, so I hadn't taken in much of the surroundings. Now, by daylight, I saw soldiers lined up along the sidewalk, with all the intersections blocked by police. We followed our PIC chaperones to our assigned shuttle buses a few blocks away. As we walked briskly down Connecticut Avenue, I couldn't get over the police and military presence. I had been expecting a high level of security and an abundance of caution, but it was still alarming to see just so many men and women in uniform, armed and standing guard. I boarded the bus, sat next to a window, and continued scanning the area. It looked as if all of DC was shut down and had been taken over by police. Looking up, I caught a glimpse of the mayor of Atlanta, Keisha Lance Bottoms, walking alongside my bus.

Surrounded by security escorts, we made our way to the Capitol building. Given the excessive military presence all around, the atmosphere looked like a scene from a war movie (or alien invasion). We were let off in front of the Capitol, then escorted along a path that led to the west side of the building, facing the Reflecting Pool and the Washington Monument. As we made our way to our seating area together, I saw Mayor Bottoms again with her husband. I'm a huge fan, and I ended up walking beside her. Though this isn't something I would normally do, I said hello and timidly asked if she would mind taking a selfie with me. She was just as gracious as I had imagined, and her eyes smiled in agreement. I took our picture, told her how much I admired her and her work, and thanked her for everything she was doing for my daughter and her family (who live in Atlanta).

When we arrived at our designated area, Derreck and I sat near each other, in the vicinity of a few others from Kamala's group. Everyone was visibly buzzing with excitement and energy, as I was. The profound significance of the event officially settled—in a far more real way than I had felt upon opening the invitation. My longtime dear friend was about to be sworn in as the first Black, first Indian, first female vice president of the United States. Though trying to maintain a sense of formality, I stood up to take a few pictures, trying to capture the moment and all the emotion surging through me. As members of the Senate arrived, the surreal nature of the experience overwhelmed me, and I sat down to just take it all in. The Obamas, Clintons, and Bushes soon took their seats. I couldn't believe I was there. It was almost too much!

Senator Amy Klobuchar, the ranking Democrat, played the role of a sort of emcee, striding up to the podium in a vibrant camel hair coat and delivering a rousing speech that got us all prepared for the monumental day we were witnessing and the long-awaited change that was about to occur. When she mentioned Madam Vice President elect, her voice rose in enthusiasm, and we all started cheering. She concluded her introduction by saying something about how, with Kamala's inauguration, little girls and boys across the world would know that anything was possible. Not for the first or the last time that day, my eyes filled with tears.

Eyeing the extraordinary crowd, I loved the literal spectrum I saw before me. I've always noticed fabric and color, and there were plenty of stunning offerings of both on the vaulted stage before me. Kamala's royal purple, Michelle Obama in deep magenta, Dr. Jill Biden in teal.

Lady Gaga, naturally, did not disappoint, making her

way to the stage in an impressive navy-and-red gown for her rendition of the national anthem. Not only melodious, she appeared and sang as if she was making a triumphant statement—and she was, especially when she gestured toward our Capitol as she declared that our flag was still there.

Finally it was time for the main event! (From my perspective at least.) Senator Klobuchar introduced Supreme Court Justice Sonia Sotomayor, noting all the firsts we were about to witness and adding that the justice was the first Latina on our Supreme Court. Kamala has always dressed with her own style of vibrant elegance. For this monumental occasion she looked especially stunning, wearing a gorgeous dress with a matching coat, the outfit enhanced by her lovely pearls. She appeared radiant, confident, and ready to get to work for the people. Doug approached, holding two Bibles up for Kamala. One had belonged to Mrs. Regina Shelton and had been brought on the plane with us all the way from Berkeley. Kamala, in honor of her spiritual godmother, had used that Bible when she was sworn in as attorney general, district attorney, and senator. The other, I later found out, was the Bible that Justice Thurgood Marshall had used for his swearing in. Like most everything else I witnessed that day, the moment was rich with intent, history, and symbolism—Thurgood Marshall was not only a civil rights activist and the first Black person to serve as a Supreme Court justice; he was also—like Kamala—an alum of Howard University.

Though the day had initially been overcast and cold, I spotted a vibrant blue sky above Kamala as she took a deep breath. I instantly choked up; tears filled my eyes. The time had come. The justice began the oath: "Please raise your right hand and repeat after me. I, Kamala..."

OMG, her name was mispronounced! *What?!* I turned to Derreck, he looked at me, and we both raised our eyebrows, playing the role of the defensive friends. I couldn't believe it. This had been a more-than-minor public issue for the past four years! It was the method some people used to intentionally try to cast Kamala as this "other." "Never mind, never mind, Stacey," I thought to myself as Kamala handled the situation with elegance and grace, smiling as she repeated her name back correctly. She wasn't going to let the significance of the moment be overridden by her name being mispronounced. (But c'mon now!) This was a historic accomplishment. After a few more glances back and forth with Derreck, I refocused.

I had been bottled up and a little anxious before that moment. But once I heard my friend say, "So help me God," my whole being relaxed, our section absolutely erupted, and from there I just allowed myself to absorb the rest of the bright and beautiful celebration.

Every scene, every act of the ceremony was imbued with symbolism, with passion, and with purpose. It was not just visually colorful but also diverse and inclusive, displaying a much-needed message to the nation: our country is vibrant and varied, and the incoming leadership was opening its arms to that range—and, by extension, to all the individuals who could see themselves represented on the stage.

I was deeply moved by Jennifer Lopez's medley of "This Land Is Your Land" and "America the Beautiful." Images from the prior administration flashed through my head—kids in cages, BLM marches across the country, white supremacists smashing the windows of our Capitol. Her impassioned voice and the words of those national secular hymns moved me to tears, which streamed from my eyes and were caught by my N95 mask. I thought of how much our country gives, but how much it takes. This was a day for celebrating the former. There was a palpable feeling of hope all around me, a refreshing energy of a new beginning.

Senator Klobuchar returned to introduce Chief Justice John Roberts, who would swear in our new president. As I saw the *enormous* family Bible that Dr. Biden hoisted up for her husband to lay his hand upon, I wondered what kind of workout routine she had done to prepare for holding that thing up! But she kept it steady as we all held our breath. We had been waiting for this transfer of power for far too long (just about four years, to be exact!). As soon as Joe Biden began repeating the oath, I both witnessed and felt the sincerity in his voice—it was obvious that he not only meant every word but also understood the responsibility of everything he was saying. It was such a relief to hear a president speak with such genuine reverence for the position.

After Kamala's swearing-in ceremony for the Senate, she had introduced me to the then–vice president. "This is my best friend from kindergarten, Stacey Johnson." His eyes widened and he flashed a big smile at me. He struck me as kind, sincere, and genuine when he shook my hand and told me how great it was to meet me. Kamala introduced him to the rest of her guests, and we all gathered around the two of them for a photograph. I don't think any of us could have imagined—as we smiled for the camera—what was in store for the two of them.

Watching him utter his oath of office, I believed him. I moved my eyes to see Dr. Biden, holding that mammoth family Bible, as she lovingly gazed up at him. From the expression in her eyes—made especially visible on the screens around us—I sensed her loving respect for her husband and all he represents. Of course nobody would know better than she did how significant that long-awaited moment was for him.

There was an audible and almost visual sigh of relief from the crowd after Joseph R. Biden completed his oath and embraced his family as "Hail to the Chief" began to play. We had a new president. Finally.

Perhaps nobody represented the renewed hope and excitement for a fresh start better than Amanda Gorman, our national youth poet laureate. Like millions around the globe, I watched in complete awe as she recited her poem "The Hill We Climb." Beyond the eloquence of her words, she was poised, dynamic, purposeful. It was impossible to divert my eyes from her performance as she gesticulated gracefully in her bright-yellow coat and red satin headband. Her poem evoked the struggles of our ancestors, hope for our youth's future, and the importance of the moment I was witnessing before me. Listening to the words, for me, also recalled the climb that Kamala had made, from being a junior prosecutor in Oakland to standing where she was now.

On top of everything else, I have a special layer of respect for Amanda Gorman, as (just like our new president, Joe Biden) she has a stutter—as does my mother, as do I. For whatever reason, when we sing, we do not stutter. I wondered if poetry had helped her overcome her speech impediment. Regardless, her fluid delivery was just one more symbolic triumph over unlikely odds and adversity.

At the conclusion of the epic ceremony our family group lingered for a while, all of us exuberant, to take a few more pictures, rejoice, and find our way back to our vehicles. We had about forty minutes to grab one of the boxed lunches and freshen up at the hotel before getting back on our buses again to attend the presidential escort and White House arrival and parade. I had never been so close to the White

House, though I've always wanted to go on a tour. The president and vice president would be arriving soon, as signaled to us by the faint sounds of marching bands in the distance. President Biden was led by a marching band from Springfield, Ohio, whereas our new vice president, always a trailblazer, and never one to forget who had supported her along the way, opted to be led by the Showtime Marching Band from Howard University, her alma mater.

I felt overcome by a heartening mix of amazement and pride as I watched the Howard band, an ensemble in every shade of Black, marching to the White House. Its music reverberated within me. The symbolism and sound felt simultaneously uplifting and profound as I looked at those young faces parading down Pennsylvania Avenue. Kamala being who she is, she managed to bring joy, to raise people's spirits, and to again show that she was not going to hesitate to give back to the communities that have supported her along her path.

All those stirring feelings were exceeded as I watched Kamala, surrounded by her family, including Maya—who saw me and waved—laughing, swaying, and saluting the masses as she made her way to her rightful place in the White House and in history. That image will stay with me forever.

After a few hours of downtime, we prepared to attend the Lincoln Memorial event and watch fireworks. The day had exceeded all expectations; I didn't think my heart could be any fuller. I couldn't even fathom that there was *more* planned for the evening, though I certainly had enough adrenaline to keep me awake.

Sitting in my hotel room, I poured a glass of Cabernet and laid out what I was going to wear for the evening's festivities. As I was reflecting on the epic day and everything I had just witnessed, my memory sent me back to early December 2019.

After a Thanksgiving holiday spent taking stock of the road ahead, Kamala had come to the painful realization that she did not see a path to winning the presidential nomination. I spoke with her on the phone, and she told me what she had openly shared with the American public: that leaving the race was "the hardest thing [she'd] ever had to do." She had given so much, and she knew how much others had given as well. We spoke briefly about the remaining candidates, and she mentioned her respect for Biden. Everything was so uncertain. I could hear the strain in her voice and sensed her exhaustion. But I watched coverage shortly after that showed how Kamala had chosen to handle withdrawing from the race after a grueling year campaigning on the road.

She didn't get on TV and start blaming other people or

other parties or bemoaning the system. She gathered her staff together at their headquarters in Baltimore, blasted Beyoncé's rendition of "Before I Let Go," and joined her crew of joyful warriors—who had worked so hard on her behalf—in a cathartic parting dance...of the electric slide. That's how she left the race: by bringing people together and finding the strength to lift them up, despite extreme disappointment. Such a significant decision is usually announced along with images of defeated campaign workers slowly emptying out of a room, leaving behind signs and buttons and whiteboard strategies that will soon be erased.

That's not Kamala's style. The first time she took the bar exam, in 1989, she didn't pass. That wasn't going to deter her—she wanted to be a lawyer, so she was going to be a lawyer. She studied for another year, kept her sights set on that goal, and passed it the following year. So it was in keeping with her nature that when she left the presidential race, she danced her way out with grace and gratitude, paused for a beat, promised to keep on fighting, then got right back up and returned to the game. That's resiliency. That's grit. And that's exactly what I had come to expect from her.

I smiled, took another sip of wine, and finished getting ready. It was time to go celebrate.

At 7:30 p.m. we all met downstairs for security sweeps before being driven to the Lincoln Memorial. The ambiance was both breathtaking and somber as spotlights illuminated the memorial and the figure of President Lincoln, looking out at the four hundred candles framing the Reflecting Pool, each one representing a thousand American lives lost to the devastating pandemic. I had seen it on television as I was getting ready, but to stand there, gazing at the poignant tribute in person, in all its dimensions, was far more heart-wrenching than I would have imagined. We paused before it in silence, all perched to the right of our new Vice President Harris as she rose before this glorious, grave scene to deliver her inaugural speech in her historic new position.

She looked every bit the class act she is in an elegant black sequined dress with black patent leather pointed-toe pumps—a style she has worn ever since we were old enough to wobble our way into wearing high heels. Her speech spoke to American aspiration. She referenced Abraham Lincoln, Dr. King, the women of our nation, and the authors of the Bill of Rights while also recognizing parents, educators, and those nurturing their communities. She delivered authenticity, poise, and unwavering optimism, saying, "Even in dark times, we not only dream, we do; we not only see what has been, we see what can be." In such words and in her voice I heard the self-confident drive she has long possessed—made that much more poignant because she was offering that confidence to America by the very act of standing there as our new vice president. That gave credence to her message that dreaming big and working hard can yield success. Her message was direct and relatable: she believes in our country and believes in what we will be able to accomplish together.

Afterward we proceeded to the steps of the Lincoln Memorial to enjoy the fireworks. The "Kamala crew" stood behind her and Doug on the stairs leading up to the Lincoln Memorial. I was so emotional, standing amid this village, this web of connections, watching our childhood friend make history right in front of me. All our profiles were alight and smiling, our eyes raised to behold the show.

When the display was finished and the crowd had thinned out, we all gathered inside the Lincoln Memorial area to take a few group photos and chat together. Though we kept a reasonable distance from each other, it felt so heartening to just reconnect with people after nearly a year of lockdowns and isolation. All too soon, we were told it was time to break up our little party. As Kamala turned to leave, I made my way to her.

"Congratulations, Kamala!"

She reached out and squeezed my hand. "Thank you, Stacey," she said. We locked smiling eyes and held that gaze for a few precious seconds, capping off one of the most meaningful days of my life.

The following day, heading back to the airport on one of the shuttle buses, Cynthia, Derreck, and I sat together in the back, recapping the past few remarkable days and discussing how amazing it was that we, her childhood friends, had been included (insofar as it was possible) in this celebration of her esteemed new position in our government.

After we boarded the plane, the captain's voice came on the overhead. She said that she and the first officer had forty-five years of combined service. In all that time, they had never been asked to do something as special and significant as fly with an all-female crew for the first female vice president. I smiled, thinking of how typical it was for Kamala to go the extra mile to make the flight memorable, meaningful, and personal.

As we flew over the country, I kept replaying scenes in my head, reflecting on Kamala, the consistency of her character, the longevity of our friendship, and all that had happened and changed over that span of time. Extraordinarily, Kamala is, in so many ways, the same person she has always been. She has never forgotten her vibrant roots, and she always finds a way to pay tribute to them. Most strikingly, she has never lost her grasp on the values that were instilled in us as children.

Kamala has never liked bullies, nor has she ever shown any hesitation or fear when standing up to them. I've seen that confidence and courage revealed since our earliest days of playing together. That grit didn't come from nowhere. Of course, the greatest inspiration was her magnificent mother. But there were others who cultivated the foundation of her character. I have been blessed enough to share common influences of that origin story.

The more I thought about the characteristics I admire most in my friend, whom I had just seen make history, the more I realized that they were the same ones that had drawn me to her throughout our childhood and had sustained our friendship. From the beginning.

Inspired, I pulled out my journal and began writing out the qualities that had defined the past few days for me. Throughout the inauguration, two words had kept echoing through my mind: *passion* and *purpose*. But there were other qualities I had seen in Kamala, ones that she has possessed throughout the long arc of our friendship.

Growing up in Berkeley at the precise moment when we did, raised by mothers who exemplified grit and ambition, surrounded by a sage, supportive, and selfless network of brilliant minds...that place and those influences remain present in her. Having shared many of the same places and personalities throughout our childhood, we forged a pure, early bond, one that gave each of us the gift of a friend for life.

Kamala has always been one to follow her dreams and fight like hell to achieve her goals. Regardless of what she's reaching toward, I trust she knows that she will always be supported from the ground up—by all of us who forged those

FRIENDS FROM THE BEGINNING

early bonds, playing together as children in the backyard at Mrs. Shelton's (whose daughters and Bible were sitting a few rows ahead of me on the plane).

Kamala has never lost her sense of joy. Even in the face of great sorrow or disappointment, she's harnessed her innate capacity to put things in perspective, let go, laugh, dance the electric slide, and move forward. On the flip side, because she's known hardship herself, her loyalty, empathy, and compassion always come through when she sees a friend—or a country, for that matter—in need. I had seen all those qualities on display from the playgrounds of our youth to the pomp and parade down Pennsylvania Avenue.

The pilot got on the loudspeaker again, interrupting my thoughts to let us know that we would soon be making our first stop. I looked out the window for a while, then instinctively smiled as I began to make out the bright landmarks that have always signaled that I'm almost home: the distinct, unmistakable peaks of the Mormon temple in Oakland; the sprawling UC Berkeley campus; its stately, soaring Campanile tower. I prepared myself to say goodbye to the Oakland crew, feeling a bit of nostalgia because I wouldn't be deplaning with them. Once we had touched down and taxied, I exchanged big, real hugs with Derreck and the Shelton daughters. With much of the plane having emptied out, I returned to my seat and gazed back out my small window.

Lifting off, I watched the lights of the city until I could no longer decipher its notable landmarks. The qualities I'd traced out on the page in front of me were indeed threads woven throughout both Kamala's and my childhood and my inauguration experience. This book looks back to the people who were essential to nurturing those characteristics. My intent is to honor the original influences Kamala and I shared, explore the places and personalities that have proven so foundational to who we are today, and give tribute to our ongoing friendship, which has lasted practically our entire lives.

To achieve this retrospective road map, I have to begin with the common ground on which we first connected: growing up in Berkeley.

Vibrance

Berkeley & Berkwood

Our hometown of Berkeley, California, sits along the east shore of San Francisco Bay, just across from the Golden Gate Bridge. For most of the world, its name alone conjures up the activism and unrest of the 1960s and 1970s and the Free Speech Movement that ignited there. Few cities are so intrinsically linked to an era and its politics. More than a half century later, people continue to associate Berkeley with that heady time of cultural expression and diversity, all forms of activism, new trends in music and food, and an overwhelming resistance to the status quo.

Much of this reputation was born and fostered around the city's branch of the University of California, the world-renowned college familiarly known as "Cal." Cal served as a natural hub, but the fight for justice—whether one's focus was racial equality, the women's movement, nuclear disarmament, or just hazy requests for peace—quickly spread beyond the campus's borders and into neighboring Oakland and San Francisco, helping cement the Bay Area's reputation as a destination for idealists and radicals of every variety.

I was born directly into this energy in 1964, right around the time when this reputation for Berkeley was gaining traction, shortly before more aggressive protests about Vietnam were launched and the Black Panthers were formed, just as the small city was garnering attention as a national, even global, hot spot for the encouragement of (and inevitable pushback against) free expression.

Though I couldn't have known it, some of the largest demonstrations opposing the war and for freedom of expression took place when I was less than one year old. I'm not a historian, but many others have cited the fall of 1964 as the most dramatic and notable turning point for Berkeley. From that point on, students and younger freedom fighters flocked to the city to be heard and seen. Being raised amid an influx of voices and movements made growing up there a unique, vibrant experience—though for me, with no basis for comparison, this environment and community were just home.

These radically shifting times affected the lives of my parents and their friends much more than mine. I didn't actively participate in demonstrations as a small child, but being exposed to them, and the issues that they raised, was unavoidable. My parents, while protective, were liberal in their child-rearing in the sense that they never discouraged me or my younger brother from asking questions or from watching and listening to the goings-on.

The larger demonstrations generally took place on and around the campus, as well as in People's Park, a notorious flash point that began as an unused university-owned parcel and became a well-trodden meeting ground for hippies and activists of the era. Located just east of Telegraph Avenue, between Haste Street and Dwight Way, People's Park was hard to miss, as were the colorful characters walking to or from the park.

I learned the park's history in the homes of my parents' friends, who were more actively engaged in the Civil Rights Movement. For a while People's Park had just been an unused lot owned by Cal. Student activists realized it was an ideal locale for a public park, and—with help from some local journalists willing to advance the campaign—local support was ignited, and it was tapped to become a sort of head-quarters for various counterculture movements. It's aptly named, as its rebirth required the assistance of hundreds of people to secure the spot, offer donations, and lay the grass, the plants, the flowers, and the trees. By the time I visited (when I was about five or six), these were all thriving, as were the Civil Rights Movement and its protests. The park became an arena for the promotion of free speech and was available to anybody who had something to say or who might be seeking out like-minded folks. Berkeley's Sproul Plaza was another gathering spot where I remember protests and rallies taking place.

Despite local efforts to use the space for open gardens and equal expression, there was obvious unrest about the project. A diverse community filled with students of all races and activists fighting for peace became a community targeted for being radical and unruly. At the time that the People's Park was literally being cultivated from the soil up, Ronald Reagan was serving as the governor of California. He opposed student demonstrations and made fervent promises to crack down on the growing activism, famously describing the Berkeley campus as a "haven for communist sympathizers, protesters, and sex deviants."

Shortly before I started kindergarten, at the tail end of the 1960s, the police cleared out much of People's Park, destroying a large section of what had been planted and putting up a fence to keep people out. That acted as a catalyst and ultimately led to a large riot between citizens and the police, one that's now referred to as "Bloody Thursday." Again, those kinds of eruptions did not directly affect me at the time, nor were they explained to me in detail. (Even if they had been, I would have been too young to understand.) But conflicts as dramatic as that would have been discussed at community gatherings, contributing to the always-lively buzz that I associate with my childhood in Berkeley.

That buzz, from where I stood, was not based in divisiveness and demonstrations. Although the town's reputation during those years involved either mobs of angry protesters or peace signs, my early memories conjure up a wider range of fascinating influences. There was an avid and very positive Back-to-Africa Movement in the early seventies, which my father used to speak about a great deal. He and his closest friends—among others in the community—consistently encouraged all of us kids to appreciate Black history and to have pride in our heritage. By the time I was becoming aware of my own identity, I was accustomed to walking down streets and enjoying the steady thumps of drum circles and jam sessions incorporating African and Cuban rhythms. But it was arguably my parents' generation that laid much of the groundwork in the early days of Berkeley's cultural vitalization, enabling me to grow up amid a diverse, inclusive community of exceptional and engaged thinkers.

———

My mother, Doris Johnson, met Shyamala Gopalan Harris at the home of Sherman Williams and Mary Lewis, a brilliant couple who were deeply entrenched in the Civil Rights

Movement. They were among the early activists who helped cultivate Berkeley's vibrant, forward-thinking, and diverse reputation. It was the summer of 1969, and Shyamala and her daughters—Kamala and Maya—were living in an apartment on Milvia Street, just a few blocks north of University Avenue. I was five years old, and Kamala was four (turning five later that year, in October).

My mom and Shyamala hit it off right away. Their primary connection was woven through me and Kamala, but they shared several crucial character traits. Both were intelligent, tough, ambitious women with minds of their own that neither was afraid to use. They were also incredibly loving and devoted mothers (and my mother still is). And they relished talking to each other. Simple phone calls or quick greetings would lead to lengthy, drawn-out conversations, which I remember best through the sound of either one laughing heartily—they shared booming, boisterous, infectious laughs—or the sight of the two of them turning away from the children to share confidences and whisper to each other.

My earliest recollections of all of us together place me and Kamala walking along Telegraph, Shattuck, and University Avenues with our mothers during the weekend as they quickly became friends. In no time at all, young Kamala and I fell in step. Together we would all shop for small, handmade things, take note of what was happening on the streets of

Berkeley, or gather for a bite to eat. We were a happy, loud, and vibrant crew, led by mothers who were both petite, but who loomed large. I'd later understand that in addition to being fiery and highly charged, they were both deeply trustworthy human beings, the kind of women people could call for sound advice. If you wanted something done right, you knew you could count on them.

It was a tremendous gift to watch Shyamala and my mom interact when I was a little girl. Through them and through other women I would grow up viewing as "aunts," I had the privilege to subconsciously absorb their model of what women could be, and should be: unabashedly strong, driven, hardworking, and courageous.

Right around the time of our moms meeting, Shyamala was looking for the ideal kindergarten for Kamala. She and my mother, who had found out about a place called Berkwood Hedge School from her cousin, discussed the progressive school, and my mom told her she was planning to send me there. Shyamala—a woman with strong intuition—liked what she had heard about it and planned to enroll Kamala at Berkwood as well. This private K–5 school sits a couple of blocks from Berkeley High School, nestled into a corner on Bancroft Way. Both in its demographics and in its educational standards, it was considered very progressive, even for that time and place.

Kamala and I began our education surrounded by a vibrant range of students who provided a strong foundation for understanding the years to come in Berkeley. When our small class would sit on the floor every morning, gathered for circle time or listening to our teachers read, we resembled some sort of diversity catalog. Our fellow classmates included (among others) Kimberly, who was Filipino; April and Anita, who were Black; and our good friend Duncan, who was white. There were children from prominent families who came from the east side and the manicured Berkeley Hills, as well as children from working-class homes who tended to journey from the "flatlands," as we called it, on the west side. At the time these distinctions bore little significance to me. Again, being raised within a culturally diverse, open-minded environment was all I knew. But they mattered to my parents, and they were one of the primary reasons I was sent to the school.

Another way that our experience at Berkwood reflected the larger foundation of growing up in Berkeley was that the school was all about encouraging freedom of expression. In addition to the basics, Berkwood offered Spanish and French (before classes in multiple languages were more commonplace). Days were filled with art and science projects and field trips. All our learning was very hands-on; we learned through experiences and activity.

Though I have assorted shards of early childhood memories, Berkwood is where my recollections really start to crystallize, right around the time when Kamala and I were playing outside on the playground. We were the friends most likely to be running around and lingering outdoors on the swings and slides. As soon as I arrived at school I would try to find Kamala. We shared only one year there together, but my memories of Berkwood are very strong. And strongest among them was the sturdy root of having met my first true best friend.

That was also the place where I learned firsthand that Kamala has no time for bullies, and no fear about telling them as much. On an especially memorable day (one I have often mentioned when asked to describe Kamala's character), our class was working with clay for an art project. We each molded our lump into whatever shape we wanted before placing it into an oven to bake and harden. When our works of art (aka lumps) were finished, they were handed back. We all stood there, delighted, admiring our amateur craftsmanship. Kamala and I were standing beside each other, comparing our work, when one of our fellow class members (a five-year-old boy behaving like…a five-year-old boy), grabbed my piece, threw it onto the ground, watched it break into pieces, and laughed tauntingly.

I was stunned, and devastated, as I looked down at my shattered piece of art, tears welling up in my eyes. Before I could launch into a full-throated wail, Kamala stepped in between me and the boy and started shouting at him, telling him exactly what she thought of his behavior. I was stunned into silence, and as multiple small heads swiveled in our direction, the little bully (also stunned, and aware there was an audience watching him) picked up a hardened piece of clay or rock and smashed it on Kamala's head, just above her eyebrow.

Her forehead started gushing blood, but she didn't recoil at all. Instead, she continued laying into the boy, demanding that he apologize to me. The teacher finally reached us to break up the fight, saw Kamala's face, and swiftly ushered her away. The gash was significant enough that the school nurse had to call Shyamala, who rushed from work to take her to the hospital. She had to get a few stitches to close the wound, and it was a bit swollen, but she came right back to school the next day, unrepentant.

That little boy never bothered either of us ever again.

Kamala still bears a very faint, tiny scar just over her eye. Though I was arguably more shaken up by the whole scene than she appeared to be, in the aftermath it made me proud, and it still does. Of course, we were only five years old at the time, but the memory of her coming to my defense has been baked into my memory, brought out, and admired countless times over the decades since. That was the moment that I realized I was blessed with a loyal, fearless friend—one who reacted instinctively to wrongdoing, who fought with her voice, and who would always have my back.

After kindergarten, Kamala left to attend Thousand Oaks Elementary School on Colusa Avenue in Berkeley—which is about two miles away from Berkwood—as did another one of our longtime, loyal, dear friends, Carole Porter. Though they weren't aware of it at our young age, they were part of the experiment to integrate Berkeley public schools through busing (a fact that Kamala famously dropped into her first presidential debate). Kamala and Carole went there from first to fourth grade. Carole later transferred to St. Joseph's Catholic Elementary School, which is where I went from first through eighth grade, and that's how she and I became close.

Kamala makes the best of things, and I believe she valued her experience at Thousand Oaks. But our educational experiences were extremely different. We knew as much because, though Kamala and I attended different schools after kindergarten, we still saw each other all the time, especially on the weekends. On the weekdays I'd often see her after school, most frequently at the Sheltons'. The tight-knit community that had been established by them, our mothers, my father, Uncle Sherman and Aunt Mary, and several others in a rotating group of other personalities enabled and encouraged our ongoing friendship. Because of that community, I never felt I had lost Kamala as a friend, and I trust she never felt she had lost me.

That community had various hubs where we'd invariably cross paths throughout those early years. When I was young, my father would pick me up from school, and he would frequently tell me we were going to stop by Uncle Sherman's, where we'd maybe hang out for an hour or an hour and a half. My mother worked full-time at the phone company, so she was less connected to the lively intellectual circles of Berkeley in the late 1960s, but my father was very involved in that scene because he and Sherman were like brothers. Uncle Sherman and Aunt Mary's Berkeley apartment sat on Woolsey Street, across the street from the Ashby BART station. Kamala and Maya would also often go there as well because, like my mom, Shyamala would have been working (in her case at the research lab). Out of the deep friendship between Shyamala and her, Aunt Mary often babysat the girls.

I have a surprisingly vivid memory of their home, given that I couldn't have been older than five or six when we first started frequenting it. I was always struck by the sheer abundance of books—overflowing from their shelves, stacked in every corner of every room, their books seemed to be the foundation of the apartment. They provided the decoration and, among the adults, were also the primary source of entertainment and discussion. Books and Berkeley were always robust subjects of conversation.

Though we continued to spend time there as we grew up, the home we'd frequent with the greatest regularity was the nursery located below Shyamala's unit on Bancroft. The nursery and building were owned by an amazing couple, Arthur and Regina Shelton. My parents' house was also an inclusive and welcoming gathering hub, but it was less convenient than the Sheltons'.

From first grade to fifth grade (when Shyamala, Kamala, and Maya left for Montreal), those homes and the friendships among our parents' community meant that not a week went by when we weren't hanging around together. In our later years of adolescence, once Kamala and her family had returned from Canada, we'd regularly spend time together at Shyamala's house in Oakland.

Weekends were especially memorable for me because my mom and Shyamala would get us together for outings. These are the events that spring to my mind most vividly, the recollections filled with bright colors and the sound of laughter. All of us would pile into Mom's 1966 forest-green Mustang: Shyamala in the passenger seat and Kamala, Maya, and I giggling together in the back. We'd take trips to Children's Fairyland or to attend movies at the Grand Lake Theatre in Oakland.

Those days were filled with happiness. I recognized that there was something very special about Kamala and Maya; they were unique. On a surface level, I had never seen anybody else my age wearing such an abundance of beautiful bracelets. They were Indian bracelets: fuchsia, yellow, teal, and other vibrant colors, framed by tiny rhinestones that glistened and jangled as we walked. I adored them, and told Kamala as much when we couldn't have been more than five years old. I remember her smiling, taking a few off her wrist, and handing them to me generously. She looked as happy to share them as I was to receive them! My eyes lit up as I slipped them onto my arms and looked at them proudly. Whenever I looked at them, they made me feel special. They were beautiful, but more importantly they were immediate symbols, and reminders of sisterhood.

On several occasions our moms took us girls to Rainbow Sign. Rainbow Sign was located on the corner of Grove Street (now Martin Luther King Jr. Way) and Derby. It had once served as a mortuary but had been converted into an extremely lively Black cultural arts center in 1971. Though it had a brief tenure, being open only until 1978, within that stretch of time it hosted some of our best-known artists, poets, writers, and dancers. They visited the center to share their stories and perform, the likes of Maya Angelou and James Baldwin gracing the space and filling it with their sage words. It was there that I first learned the lyrics to "Lift Every Voice and Sing," widely considered the Black national anthem. There would always be food, music, and dancing. More than intricate details of the venue, I remember the energy felt in the space. There was a sense of joy and openness all around us. It was a vibrant place of celebration filled with people of all ages and backgrounds, gathered together for solidarity and for the pride and pleasure one felt there.

One of the great bonds between my mom and Shyamala was their shared love for art, music, and dance. They also both clearly loved exposing us kids to that world, and to the rich diversity that was celebrated not just at Rainbow Sign but throughout Berkeley and the wider East Bay. On one occasion we all went to a Kwanzaa celebration near West Oakland. Kwanzaa, which is celebrated each year from December 26 to January 1, is a holiday created by Maulana Karenga in 1966 as a celebration of African heritage and unity. I remember listening carefully as it was explained to me. Kwanzaa honors seven principles of our heritage: unity, self-determination, collective work and responsibility, cooperative economics, purpose, creativity, and faith. These core values and this vibe were felt at Rainbow Sign for sure, but they were also characteristics shared and encouraged by our community and its pillars: Aunt Mary and Uncle Sherman, the Sheltons, Shyamala, and my parents.

————

Right around when we were going into the sixth grade, Shyamala secured a job working in research at McGill University, in

Montreal. My mom often spoke about missing spending time with Shyamala, and either with Sherman and Mary or over the dinner table, she and my dad would discuss how she and the girls were doing, all on their own, so far away from home. My concept of time wasn't the same as the adults'. As soon as school ended for the summer, Kamala would be back for the holidays, and we would be immediately in each other's company, so her absence never felt so long as to cause a fracture in our friendship. In addition to the summers, I'd see her throughout most vacations or breaks. To my mind, because we were so young, nothing really changed between us in terms of our relationship and connection. That has proven true throughout our lives: as soon as we're back together, the time away from each other seems irrelevant.

She never complained about the move, though it couldn't have been easy. I'm sure they found a way to make Canada an adventure, and she reflects upon it as a great experience. All that varied exposure to different worlds—with holidays either in India or, more often, back home in the Bay Area—adds depth to a person like Kamala, who always finds a way to carve out her own space and make a group of friends. I presume it must have strengthened her ability to connect with all different types of people, which of course has served her well as a public figure and a politician. My mom stayed in relatively close touch with Shyamala, through regular letters and the occasional boisterous phone call, so she would always know when they were heading home.

While I don't remember her absence ever being an issue, her presence was always an event and a source of delight. Anytime Mom checked the calendar or hung up the phone and let me know that Kamala and Maya would be coming back to Berkeley for a trip, I felt as if Santa Claus were making a special off-season visit. I'd march through our home with excitement, telling my dad (as though he hadn't just heard it), "Kamala will be here on Friday!" I can so easily call back the happy anticipation I would feel running up the stairs of their unit on Bancroft, or later—when Shyamala bought her first house on Turnley Avenue—driving with excitement into the East Oakland hills.

Once reunited, we would go to parks and parties, or simply stroll down Telegraph or walk to the Ashby BART station flea market. We were always active, always going out and seeing people and exploring the city. Whenever she came back to the East Bay, I'd introduce her to any friends I had made in her absence. Kamala never flinched at meeting new people, and before I knew it, she would have created relationships of her own with them. I never minded in the slightest—just the opposite. She remained among my very best friends, and it felt like a gift and point of pride to introduce her to any new friends. Our bond was sealed.

Much of that welded connection can be attributed to the ineffable gifts of our childhood in Berkeley. I think back on it like a precious, special extended moment, filled with high-octane laughter, warmth, color, and familiarity. I cherish that community and am proud of the extent to which it sits at the foundation of who I am. Those early years of my life have an almost elastic quality, in the sense that they—and the community that defined them—continue to hold Kamala and me together, bound by the core values that were impressed upon us from as early as kindergarten. It makes our bond that much stronger that our connection was initiated by our decisive mothers, just as they were forming their own friendship.

Grit

Mothers

Anybody who has ever heard Kamala speak, to an audience large or small, has learned that her greatest source of inspiration is her mother. I too feel immensely blessed by the love and continued friendship I share with my own mother, Doris. These remarkable, giving women brought us into the world and, while blazing trails of their own, proved to us that we should never underestimate ourselves (or them, for that matter).

Doris Johnson, née Bradley, is phenomenal. She is the toughest little fighter I know—diminutive only in height. Though she stands about four feet and eleven inches tall, her spirit is filled to the brim with brilliant, feisty determination. As far as the stories go, her petite frame has always contained a massive spirit—one that I have never seen back down from a challenge.

My grandparents were progressive in the sense that they

wanted her to understand the world around her and the challenges she would face. They would read *Negro Digest* magazine (later renamed *Black World*), then inform the children about what was going on and how people of color were being treated. She heard them talk about W. E. B. Du Bois, Carter G. Woodson, Black history in America, and various acts of racism. My mother, who has an astonishingly sharp memory, still remembers being a little girl and asking my grandmother, "Why do white people treat us so bad?" Nearly eighty years later, she repeats her mother's response: "Well, Doris…there's more good than bad, otherwise we'd still be in shackles."

She moved through her early years operating under those devastating standards but finding some comfort trusting that there was more good than bad on a broad scale. On a personal level, one of her greatest challenges was her stutter. The speech impediment runs in our family, shared by my mom, her sister, her son (my first cousin), my brother, and me.

It had its consequences. When Mom was thirteen or fourteen years old, she and her good friend Marion Bell were hall monitors. During classes, students had to have a pass from their teacher to go from one hall to another. As she recalls it, one day a "big white chick" came directly up to her (as she was smaller than Marion), and tried to bully Doris into letting her enter the hallway that led to the offices of the principal and other staff members. "No, not without a pass," Mom said resolutely. This girl was incensed and tried to threaten her, calling her the N-word.

So, never one to accept an ignorant slur...my mom jumped her.

The fight was quickly broken up, and the two girls were dragged into the office of the white principal of Harry Ells Junior High School. He asked to hear both sides of the story. My mom, feeling anxious and incensed, stuttered badly trying to get out her version, which was the truth. He interrupted her: "Why, this girl needs speech therapy!" He suspended my mom and let the other girl (the bully) go back to class. My grandmother, from whom my mother inherited much of her fighting spirit, was not one to let such matters go without making herself heard. She came to the school to have words with the principal. By means unknown, the white girl's boyfriend somehow got involved in the discussion. In response, a tall Black kid who was friends with Doris said, "Well, if *he's* in it, then I'll get in it!" A brawl ensued in the hallways, and other kids joined in. According to my mom, there was practically a small race riot over that hall pass incident.

The principal took Doris out of her favorite class, sewing, and put her in a speech class—which, in the end, was actually to her benefit. The teachers taught her how to relax and breathe, almost as if preparing herself to reach a meditative state. The instructor told my mom that she thinks faster than she talks and taught her how to slow down her thoughts, or at least think before speaking. Because I suffer from a stutter as well, I notice it to this day when Mom slows down or pauses midsentence to avoid stuttering and clearly articulate her thoughts.

I'm proud of her for overcoming that personal obstacle, especially knowing that she did so at a time when there was very little room for her to slip up or appear less capable of articulating herself. Beyond the challenges of her life, and perhaps because of them, Mom has nurtured a very firm and evolved sense of right and wrong. She knows precisely how well she deserves to be treated and has always been steadfast in sticking to that. Though she no longer responds by jumping someone, you can be sure that she'll hold people accountable if they disrespect her in any way.

Doris never took anything for granted, nor did she accept limitations or assume that her life choices should be determined by anybody other than herself. Her accomplishments began at a young age, as she was very active in school. In high school she was a member of the Student Government Committee, Advisory Committee, and Boosters Club. At age fifteen, in 1951, she became the school's first Black cheerleader (or "Yell Leader," as they were called). I learned long ago that I should not make assumptions about or put words into the mouth of my mother, who also happens to be my number one "Yell Leader" in life. When I asked her about her experience in high school, she replied:

I was fifteen and had just entered the tenth grade at El Cerrito High School. Your dad and I had gotten back together, after I forgave him for not coming to my twelfth birthday party. I asked him why he and his friends hadn't come. He claimed he didn't know [about it]. I told him, "Oh yes you did, I told you! I invited you guys." Well, anyway ... he and I and other friends were at the football game. I saw these white girls as cheerleaders. I said to myself, "I can do that—and I want to do that!" We had all these Black guys out there playing football, basketball, baseball (some became famous, like Pumpsie Green), and yet there was not one Black girl cheering them on.

In the fall when we voted to select our new student body, I decided to run for Yell Leader. It was an elected position. All the white girls divided up in their own groups. "That's not going to stop me," I said. I got my best friends, Mittie Ann Wheeler and Dolores McShane, to get out there with me, and I taught them one of the yells. We practiced every day, then we got in front of the whole student body when I ran for the position. I took the mic and introduced myself, explained why I was running, and told everyone to vote for me. And they did! (After I won, your dad told me that one white guy told him he voted for me simply because I had the guts to get out there and run.)

It was a lot of fun! It made me part of the Student Body Office. I really enjoyed cheering for the teams and leading the crowds, especially when I was cheering for your dad when he was playing basketball. After the game I would wait outside the gym doors while he took his shower. Then he would walk me home. We'd walk down to San Pablo and catch the bus to my house.

It was fun leaving class early so we could ride with the teams to various schools that we were playing against. We won most of our games. One night game at Piedmont High School, which was a predominantly white school, some student got my pom-pom while it was on the ground, and he pulled all the long streamers off of it—I knew it was racially motivated. I got over it. And though I didn't know it at the time, I had opened the door for other students of color. The following year a Black guy, John, ran and won. I was just so happy for him.

Though she was a skilled Yell Leader, Doris's dream had always been to become a fashion designer. She'd learned how to sew from her maternal grandmother, who had a sewing machine. My mom has always been very focused, very driven. Once she knew her life goal, she made plans accordingly. In high school she took journalism classes with a mind to using the knowledge as a fashion editor. She took commercial art so she could design fashion ads for newspapers. And she took French, envisioning herself one day visiting the legendary fashion houses of Paris. She was well on her way after graduating from high school. She designed and created many of her own clothes, then began displaying her work in shows around the Bay Area, using her good friend Carolyn as one of her models.

But she was also very mindful of her parents and tended to follow their counsel. While she had been curating all the skills necessary to become a fashion designer, they urged her to look out for herself and "get a *good* job"—in other words, one with steady pay and benefits. So after marrying my father and having me, she finally let go of her dream of becoming an international designer. (Don't get me wrong; she's still a veritable fashionista, and we love to sew and go shopping together to this day.)

She started working for the phone company, which was Pacific Telephone and Telegraph Company or PT&T, later Pacific Bell. She was hoping to achieve the stability that her parents felt was so essential. There, as everywhere else, she thrived—though nothing was handed to her. She was initially hired as a long-distance operator, but quickly advanced to engineer, which was a rare ascension for women, and particularly for women of color. She battled her way through unrelenting racism and sexism throughout her entire career.

Many years later I would follow in her footsteps when I started working for Pacific Bell as a telephone operator. Though I've seen no shortage of discrimination throughout my decades making my own way up the ladder, it brings me great pride that it was pioneers like my mom who helped normalize the presence of Black women in typically male work environments. She has always been sharp, with a phenomenal memory, a healthy store of curiosity, and a capacity for swiftly understanding new systems. She never liked it when people made assumptions about her or tried to talk over her, though she endured plenty of such treatment. And again, given that I have the great blessing of still being able to just pick up a phone and ask her to refresh my memory, she will share her own story:

My mother and father always told me, "Nobody is better than you, and you're no better than anybody else. You're equal." Just after I got hired to work at the phone company, back in the fifties, my mom and dad sat me down. They told me, "You know you're going to have to work twice as hard as anybody else, right?" I nodded. Yes, I knew that. Then Daddy said, "But don't ever let any man (and I knew exactly who he was talking about: white men) make you think that they're better than you are. Because they're not. Nobody is better than you are, and you're no better than anybody." That's what he'd say, over and over.

He also used to always advise me, "Remember, if you get stabbed, they'll bleed just like you do." Off I went. And I had to fight. Racism. Sexism. Oh my God. You name it, from 1955 all the way up to 1985. Men were always saying silly stuff trying to be funny, you know the kind, when it's actually not funny? Like, even the way they would say, "You know, Doris, I respect you . . ." was just so condescending. I expect to be respected! I don't play those games. What do they want me to say? "Oh, thank you"? Whenever I would get one of those comments I would just repeat what my daddy had said. "You're no better than me and I'm no better than you. If I cut you with a knife, you will bleed just like me." Oh boy. These guys would look at each other like, "Hmm . . . this one might cut us!"

I got interested in engineering when I was working long distance—I wanted to know what was behind the switchboard. How is it possible that, just by pressing a button and counting, "One thousand, two thousand," you can be connected to a voice across the country? It's still amazing to me. It is.

I was the only Black person in the whole building in San Francisco on Bush Street. At that point they put me in the long-distance department because I already had experience, while the other girls that were with me, the white girls, were all in information—meaning 411—or operators.

I advanced from long distance and I went to TWX—which is still an operator, but on teletype—still with the Pacific Telephone and Telegraph Company. I took a lot of calls from the FBI and sensitive things like that. We only dealt with businesses, the FBI, and picture calls (what we now think of as a fax or a scan). If you were taking those kinds of sensitive calls with the FBI, you'd have to put a clamp over the keys so that you weren't leaving anything open or vulnerable to being intercepted. It was really, really interesting work.

I loved it, but I wanted to do more. And I had to get out of there, because I didn't like the way I was being treated. I knew that I was just as good as any man, but that's not how I was dealt with. I'll never forget this one day . . . it was just about five o'clock, which would be when you would put up a red card on your position so the chief operators or supervisors would know that there were no calls coming in. It was five minutes to five, no calls coming out on the board, so I took my glasses off. I had a cord in my hand, just in case a call did come in. I was twirling my glasses, and the district plant manager—who's like a division supervisor—came just struttin' in, wearing his wing-tip shoes. All you have to do is look at their feet. If you see those wing-tip shoes? Oh my. You know what those men are all about.

So he comes swaggering over and sits right down at the supervisor's desk, even though she was there! She got up. I never did like that kind of business—you know, "Here I am, the king." Please. He's sitting in her seat, and she's standing. And do you know what he did, Stacey? He plopped his feet right up on her desk! On all of her things! Oh my. So then he looks over at me and says to her, even though he could have easily addressed me, "Go tell that girl to either put her glasses on or to put them away." "That girl." And she actually came over and repeated that! That kind of behavior just made me so mad.

That's when I became determined to get out of there. I didn't have time for that! I put in for a transfer . . . and I got it. I could not believe it. It was very, very hard to get out of that department, because they always needed operators. So I got the transfer, but first I had to be interviewed. Three white men . . . again.

I got myself all prepared, went in, and sat down in a room. Just me and the three of them. I looked down: wing-tip shoes. Oh Lord. "Here we go," I thought. So two of them were asking me all of these questions, like, "Why would someone like you want to come over to engineering?" Those kinds of questions. But I said to myself, "I am not going to let these men intimidate me." My goal was to get out of being a telephone operator, which I had only planned on doing for two years. I was on a career path! I wanted to be an engineer; I wanted to be a manager.

One of the guys' last name was Shattuck—and I'll never forget this. Here I am, twenty or twenty-one years old, and *he came over and put his foot on the chair beside me and leaned in. Just trying to intimidate me. He was one of the two men that were standing up, while I was just sitting there, responding, trying to be as clear as possible.*

But there was also an older man, who was sitting down behind them. He didn't have much to say at all, but I could tell he was listening closely. I had my story together, and I explained very clearly. "I'm fascinated by the telephone network, and all I want to do is to learn how the system works." Which was true. The older man just looked at me and finally asked one question, at the end of the whole interview: "Sounds like you really like engineering, huh?"

"Oh yes, yes I do." That was all. And I got hired. Once I was in the department, I found out his name was Mr. Goff. He was actually the district manager—those other two reported to him, even though they had been the ones coming in like they were some kind of big shots. Nah. But me and Mr. Goff, we ended up getting along really, really good. He respected me, and I respected him.

Though she was always determined and driven to succeed independently, Mom has always enjoyed helping other people. She started doing this at Pacific Bell, where she helped organize and contribute to food drives. She also became a mentor to a man named Tom Sykes, a technician who worked in the Central Office. She recognized that he was a smart young

Black man who took initiative. Knowing the hurdles that would be placed before him, she set out to encourage him and to clear the way for him to become an engineer manager, which he eventually did. She's very proud of that.

Somehow, between hard work and attentive mothering, she still found the time to also become the first Black program chairwoman of the Society of Women Engineers (SWE) in San Francisco during the 1970s. She was asked to join the Golden Gate Section, which was a professorial branch. (The collegiate sections were based in UC Berkeley and San Francisco State University and as far north as Santa Rosa.) Founded in the 1950s, the society had (and still has) a mission to stimulate women to achieve careers as engineers and leaders, empowering them to succeed, move up the ladder, and be recognized for their work in a traditionally male-dominated field. Mom was part of its career guidance program, which meant she would go into high schools around the Bay Area, speaking to the students about what it was like to be an engineer.

The society's meetings would have various speakers. When she was serving as the program's chairwoman, which I know she enjoyed immensely, she got to plan the monthly meetings and arrange for various speakers to come and talk to the SWE. She really enjoyed Bella Abzug—who helped found the National Women's Political Caucus—when she came to speak with them in 1979. Being involved with the society was a great way to meet like-minded, fascinating people who shared her work and expertise. She was later asked to be the treasurer, and for a while served as the first Black treasurer for the society. So she was always doing something, always active and engaged, blazing new paths and helping others along the way.

Throughout my childhood Mom was the queen of DIY, and she would head off to Berkeley's Tool Lending Library whenever anything needed to be fixed. For life's inevitable administrative tasks, she would generally go to Uncle Sherman, who somehow was always available to provide her (and anyone who needed it) with legal advice. After he passed away, she discovered the Law Library in downtown Oakland, where attorneys would offer free legal advice on the first Saturday of the month. When one of my childhood friends lost her father and was overwhelmed with legal matters, Mom just stepped in, picked her up, and marched her over to get advice and counsel from the attorneys. That's the kind of person she is: when she sees a need, she does whatever she can to help take care of it.

From the late 1960s through the mid-1970s, Mom was also a member of Las Electras, a women's club that met once a month at a member's house. They rotated as hosts and would use their time together to come up with fundraising events for various charities that might be especially in need during a given time. Though she worked constantly, Las Electras was another important outlet for her, one that allowed her to remain active and engaged in the community, offering support in one way or another. Maintaining friendships has always been a priority in Doris's life, and she consistently kept up her relationships with close girlfriends and found ways to surround herself with women like her, which is to say women who were supportive, loyal, and willing to lend a hand. They also all shared the capacity to hold on to these lifelong friendships, which is a quality I took note of and have always prioritized in my own life.

Shyamala's work took her to very different places from my mom. Their day-to-day lives bore few similarities. But they both entered fields where people were unaccustomed to seeing women of color, and they both relished what they did. They were also both highly resourceful. These women took care of business and got the job done ... no matter what that job was.

When my mom first met Shyamala, she admired how beautiful and thick her long braid was, swinging nearly at her waist. Doris was interested in learning about the red bindi on her forehead and took note of how well Shyamala dressed—something I would later appreciate and admire. Sometimes she'd wear bright colors, sometimes muted, but she was always assembled with elegance and poise.

Shyamala and Aunt Mary were extremely close. My mother didn't go out with them all that much, nor did she see Shyamala consistently over the years. But their mutual respect and enjoyment was obvious whenever they were in each other's company. Shyamala was a serious woman with an intense personality. That intensity didn't manifest itself in a cold or harsh fashion. Her presence was powerful, but softened with great warmth and a great capacity for humor. Whenever Kamala's mother and mine did connect, there was no way of stopping their chatting and noticeably loud laughter. My mother paid attention to Shyamala and her recommendations. She still recalls when Shyamala came by the house and had cut off all her waist-length, thick hair. Kamala and Maya were there too.

"Wow, *Shyamala*, I just love your haircut!" Doris exclaimed. Shyamala smiled and turned around, showing my mom the tapered back. My mom thought it looked fabulous and really complemented her face. "Who cut your hair?"

"A man named Randy. He works in Jack London Square. Let me get you his number," Shyamala said. Soon after, my mom started going to Randy as well. She always wore a short cut with wispy bangs, and she had been looking for someone good to maintain her tapered cut. She loved it, and both women wore similar haircuts from then on. Doris insists he was the only person who could dye her hair its exact natural color. Randy moved to a shop in downtown Oakland on Nineteenth Street, and they both continued going to him for years, until he relocated to Palm Springs.

Although their relationship stayed centered around us children, whenever our moms took us out—to the parks, to Oakland's Children's Fairyland, to Kwanzaa festivals, or to movies at the Grand Lake Theatre—they wouldn't stop talking for hours at a time. My mom loved being around other career-driven mothers, and the two of them felt free to confide in each other about their experiences, be they work related or centered around their personal lives.

My parents were quite the socialites, and due to my dad's connections, they would take advantage of all the hip places on offer in Berkeley, around the East Bay, and across the bridge in San Francisco. My mother had no shortage of stories to offer about gigs they had gone to around the Bay Area. Shyamala, who would spend many late hours working, on occasion would call my mom to ask, "Do you mind if I drop off the girls for a few hours?" When she would come to pick up Kamala and Maya, I always knew we had plenty of time left to play, as our moms always enjoyed the opportunity to catch up. Shyamala would get very excited telling my mom all about her research and the different breakthroughs she and her colleagues were making. My mom just loved learning about them, as well as hearing Shyamala talk about intriguing spots she had visited—this brand-new wonderful little restaurant called Chez Panisse, on Shattuck Avenue, or the places she had been on a very well-deserved trip to Paris. But none of those fascinating places would get her as animated as talking about being in the lab. Shyamala was deeply passionate, fueled by the ambition to do nothing less than find a cure for cancer. Unprompted, she would look at my mom and simply say, "I love my job." She did. With Shyamala's combination of intelligence and courage, my mom always said she could have worked at any university in the world. Doris appreciated how important Shyamala's work was for her, and she never tired of trying to grasp her breakthroughs.

I loved how much she and my mom enjoyed and innately understood each other through the grit of their work ethic. But she was my mom's friend; Kamala was my friend. Though I was around her all the time, Shyamala and I never had an independent relationship. We girls would be talking, laughing, doing whatever we were doing. Our moms would be on one side of the kitchen and we'd be on the other.

Shyamala was, however, very influential to me in terms of spreading both Indian and African cultural awareness and pride. She did this for her daughters—of course—but generously spread that knowledge throughout our whole community. I saw the most evidence of and emphasis on this in the clothes and jewelry she and the girls wore, the vivid art throughout all their homes, and the books on their shelves. Her knowledge about both cultures was vast, and she would share it generously.

After the family left for Canada, whenever they came back for holidays or the summer Doris and Shyamala wasted no time. They would instantly reconnect, just like Kamala and me. No matter how much time might have passed since we had talked or seen each other, we picked right up from where we'd left off. Later in life, in the late 1970s and into the eighties, my mother and I would spend time at Shyamala's house in Oakland. It seemed that everybody would gather there, especially around the holidays. Whenever Shyamala's brother and sisters came to visit from India, the whole crew would go to her house and enjoy a scene filled with music, plates and plates and more plates of food, loud talking, and vibrant colors. Doris and Shyamala would find each other, something I might not see through the crowd but could always hear.

Over time, Doris and Shyamala would go far longer stretches without contact, but their respect for each other's grit had long since solidified, and they would invariably find something to laugh about together. Once again, their model played a role in my friendship with Kamala, as—at least for me—the two of them revealed that sisterhood is durable, reliable, and enduring.

Wisdom

The Village

While Doris and Shyamala's friendship was largely centered around us, most of our community's connections (including the initial meeting between our mothers) can be traced back to Uncle Sherman and Aunt Mary. They had been crucial players at the height of Berkeley's civil rights era and were regarded as deeply knowledgeable, dependable human beings. When it came to advice and education, they were the very definition of pillars in our community.

Their personalities differed, but their strengths were similar: both were highly intelligent and skilled at delivering brief, punchy responses, as well as always ready to offer commentary and counsel to those who asked for it. A couple for more than fifty years, Mary was a professor and Sherman was an attorney and a family lawyer. To be honest, I don't know how he ever turned a profit, considering the extent of his pro bono work, which is all I ever witnessed him doing. He was a lawyer for the people, for our community. My mom was among the many people who preferred going to Uncle Sherman for sound legal advice, because he'd give it to her straight and was especially good at cutting through legalese and putting matters in plain terms. When we'd drop by their home, Sherman was often in front of his typewriter, on the phone talking to his clients, or heading off to go visit clients in their homes. Sometimes he went to Ron Dellums's office, where a lot of young lawyers worked.

Uncle Sherman and Aunt Mary were an incredibly valuable, definitive cornerstone. As individuals, and all the more so as a couple, they were among the most brilliant people I've ever encountered. I don't recall them as being especially social, meaning they wouldn't go out a great deal... but they didn't really need to: people came to them (or Sherman would be at our house, then weaving through clients' homes in the neighborhood). They were humble people who applied their means and energy to helping others.

That selflessness was embedded into their natures, and they instilled that ethos in all those in their orbit. Their modest home was filled with books and with music, especially jazz, which Uncle Sherman was always playing—an instant connection between him and my father, both in their friendship and in my memory. Together, Aunt Mary and Uncle Sherman underscored the importance of looking out for others—especially within our Berkeley community.

*   *   *

Uncle Sherman, born and raised in New Orleans, was particularly present throughout my youth. Just as with my mom, Shyamala, and Aunt Mary, his stature belied his larger-than-life presence. I have countless recollections of all five feet and five inches of him walking briskly through our house, from the living room to the den—where my dad would usually be—or quickly popping his head into the kitchen to say hello to my mom and have a little chat. His gait suggested a man who always had something to get done, which is the pace I envision when I remember him striding out to his car, a little gray Toyota Corolla.

Daddy and Sherman had met shortly after they got out of the service, around the late 1950s. My father had been in the air force, while Sherman had served in the army. They truly were like brothers, which is why Sherman's was among the most consistent presences of my youth. In the early years of my life, he stopped by our home almost every day—almost as if he were doing the rounds through the neighborhood—or my dad would bring us over to Uncle Sherman's.

If a day went by when we didn't catch a glimpse of him, he was missed. We'd usually see him just before dinnertime. If my dad was making dinner on that particular day, which was generally the case, he would get a kick out of impressing Sherman with whatever he had going on the stove. My dad loved to cook, and he loved to eat. He would tell Uncle

Sherman how he'd just finished "burnin'," or how "mean" (in other words, delicious) his dinner was going to be. Uncle Sherman never stayed very long, maybe only thirty minutes or so, just enough time to check in with my dad about what was going on in the community and see how we were all doing. He'd stay a little longer if a game was on and would sit and watch for a while with my dad. In those cases they'd have a drink—Dad would have a beer, and Sherman would more than likely be holding a barrel glass with a shot of brandy or cognac. He would sit and swirl it, laughing and sharing commentary with Daddy, or they might pause in their chatter to put on a jazz album. So many flashes of memory over the years deliver the two of them sitting and listening to Miles or Coltrane, often while flipping through books.

They had a very special bond, with a mutual respect that was as obvious as it was heartwarming. They engaged with each other like the best of family: with aligned senses of humor, capable of saying the least number of words that would trigger long hearty laughs. If they weren't discussing Berkeley culture, their conversations revolved around athletes, politics, and books—always books.

Uncle Sherman was one of only two of my dad's friends who ever could, or would, lecture or try to impart wisdom to me and my brother. (The other was his great friend Bobby Morehead, whom my brother and I also referred to as Uncle.) *Lecture* is not quite accurate, as Uncle Sherman never spoke

down to us, or to anybody. But he had a way of talking—
like my dad—that made you want to listen and try to learn.
He was clear and often delivered profound, simple statements, urging us to do the right thing and stay on track in
our lives.

He regularly spoke to us about the importance of improving on the last generation's success. In her speeches Kamala
often acknowledges standing on the shoulders of those who
came before us. When I hear the line, or any similar refer-
ence, I think of Uncle Sherman. He expected greater things
from us than from his generation, and he expected our children to be greater than us.

After making such statements, Uncle Sherman would
follow with a strong, sharp "Hmm!" This familiar grunt,
delivered with force from the depths of his diaphragm, served
as either a question or a statement, depending on whether you
were prepared to engage in an intellectual debate. Regardless
of the exchange, Uncle Sherman's emphatic "Hmm!" made
you think! He was always right, and the older I got, the more
I became aware of that.

In terms of our relationship, his avuncular role probably
reached its greatest frequency later in my life, during the
weeks when he and my dad teamed up to advise me on all
the pros (*never* the cons) of going to UC Berkeley. I was set
on going to UC Davis, but that wasn't good enough for the
two of them. Neither understood why I would do such a thing

when I could just stay at home and take the bus or bike up the hill to Cal.

Uncle Sherman felt the same way about Kamala going to Howard. Why was she going to go across the country when Cal—the alma mater of both of her parents (for graduate school) was right here? Cal was where Uncle Sherman and Aunt Mary had fallen in love and where they had met Shyamala and Kamala's father, Donald. My parents were not originally part of that close-knit group, but as soon as Uncle Sherman met my dad, he brought him (and our family) into their strong, tight circle.

Uncle Sherman's kindness to our family and to us kids extended beyond that initial connection and revealed itself in many forms throughout my life. I'd be running in a track meet and would look up and spot him there, cheering and just being supportive. He'd do the same once my brother, Ronny, started playing football. He genuinely cared about the youth in the community—that was all a part of his desire to encourage the next generation and set a model for continuing that tradition. He treated Kamala, Maya, Ronny, and me like flesh-and-blood relatives. There was nothing he wouldn't do to help us become the best versions of ourselves. He was a positive force, a joyful, sage, and supportive presence for young people in particular.

He had an especially close bond with Kamala and Maya, who would often be over at his house. Uncle Sherman taught

Kamala how to play chess and would smile lovingly at her, with a knowing glint in his eye, while they were playing. She often cites his influence in helping her think strategically. I would occasionally mess around with the set, but chess never stuck for me—instead, Mom and I loved to play jacks and checkers together.

Uncle Sherman wanted the best for us and never shied away from sharing his thoughts on how we might go about achieving that. Ronny remembers Uncle Sherman for always valuing intelligence over money and making it clear that "success is measured by how often you help others." He was pro-Black and very devoted to seeing racial progress in Berkeley. Along with Aunt Mary and her brother Freddy, he made sure to bring such issues to the forefront of our awareness.

I'm not one to dwell on regrets, but one that I do have is that I never got to know Aunt Mary in the same way I knew Uncle Sherman. I still referred to her as Aunt, in large part because she and Shyamala were like sisters, just as my dad and Sherman were like brothers. That's how we were lucky enough to grow up supported by an enforced web of brilliant minds and interconnected families.

During their student years, Sherman, Mary, and Shyamala were part of a highly intellectual circle of friends that included Mary's brother Freddy. Freddy didn't play as central a role in my young life, but he was very often in the mix of our community. My father knew him better than my mother did, and he was Uncle Freddy to Kamala and Maya. To us kids he was always kind and thoughtful. Collectively, they had been sincerely motivated to create change and highly engaged on campus as well as off campus in the community.

Aunt Mary's demeanor was that of an academic, which she was, through and through. Her academic résumé was unbelievably impressive, though as a child I wasn't fully aware of the scope of it. In fact, I wouldn't learn the whole extent of her life's achievements until after she passed away. But she and Freddy used to invite people to get together during the earliest stages of the Black Consciousness Movement in the East Bay. Their house on Harmon Street in Berkeley served as an intellectual salon and a headquarters of awareness of sorts, one where people would congregate to share ideas and strategies for protest while forming thick bonds of friendship. Over time their discussion group evolved and broadened to include well-known poets, writers, artists, and other leaders in the Black community. The likes of Fannie Lou Hamer, LeRoi Jones (Amiri Baraka), and Maya Angelou would frequent their home. Shyamala would have been one of the few non-Black attendants at those meetings, but she never struck me as uncomfortable with being the first or being the only—and of course she raised her daughters with that level of self-confidence.

Aubrey LaBrie—Shyamala and Mary's very close friend

and Mrs. Shelton's nephew—later shared these Harmon Street memories and knowledge with me. He spoke with particular animation about an afternoon when Malcolm X came to Mary and Freddy's house to meet with a large crowd of students and admirers, many of whom were hoping to form a new Black political movement. Aunt Mary had received her PhD in anthropology from the University of Washington after spending two years in Ghana, where she'd conducted research on the culture of market women. Aunt Mary was modest, never one to boast. But she was extremely proud of—and not afraid to share—the fact that the dissertation committee had signed off on her work without any corrections or even suggestions for changes.

Once she became Dr. Mary Lewis, she taught at San Francisco State University, where she was always at least engaged in, if not at the forefront of, student demonstrations and negotiations that ultimately led to the establishment of the Black Studies Department. She was then invited to participate in the "experimental college" within that department. Its purpose was to develop courses relevant to what was going on within the Black community at the time. Along with Aubrey, she was also approached by student government at San Francisco State to develop its Black Studies program.

She moved on to teach at California State University, East Bay, and later joined the faculty of Laney College as an adjunct professor, where she taught all the way up until

May 2012, serving as chairwoman of the African American Studies Department for several semesters. Aunt Mary taught a variety of courses, most of them revolving around Black political science and history, including a course on the Black family and another she called the Black Experience through Film. She pioneered Laney College's popular Women of Color class, which she co-taught with Asian and Latina colleagues. At Laney she helped lead the Project Bridge program, a highly regarded project for adults seeking to take mainstream college courses.

Her trailblazing efforts at Laney were noticed, and she was invited to teach at Contra Costa College in San Pablo, where she offered courses in African American studies, cultural anthropology, and, at one point, even mathematics. Through the study-abroad program at Contra Costa College, she accepted an assignment to teach in Osaka, Japan (a country that was always of special interest to her, Sherman, Freddy, and my dad). She absolutely loved it, considering the experience one of the highlights of her life. For several years she remained in close contact with some of her students from Osaka, continuing to mentor and advise them long after her project had ended.

As a child I had little idea of the extent of what she had done, what she was doing, or how accomplished she was. She wasn't the type of woman who felt the need to promote herself. Aunt Mary also wasn't easy to get to know—which is not to suggest she was ever cold or aloof by any measure. But she didn't offer personal information freely. Instead, she observed. She listened a lot and she listened closely, always taking notice of people, not in a strange way, just out of genuine curiosity and interest. She didn't have the same kind of gregarious, voluminous tendencies that Daddy and Uncle Sherman shared, but her presence was always noted. She was a woman of integrity and intelligence, and when I was over there, she was often weaving in and out of the room, occasionally chiming in to offer her opinion.

In addition to being a scholar, Mary was an unbelievable seamstress and had an impressive range of beautiful fabrics, some of which she had brought back from Ghana. Perhaps because of my mom's passion and my own, I noticed that she would often be sewing when we visited. Still, she was always listening to the surrounding conversations, and she could definitely hold her own—and enjoyed doing so—in the loftier or more topical debates that might catch her interest, or whenever the conversation involved books that intrigued her.

Though quiet, she always had a generous smile to offer young people, making it evident that she cared for us. She would ask earnest questions when we were children and during our teens, usually revolving around how school was going and what we were interested in academically. Aunt Mary was very socially aware and serious about us applying ourselves. The intimidation I occasionally felt in her presence was due to a feeling that she could see right through me and intuitively knew when I might not have been, say, studying as long and hard as I should have been.

But it wasn't all about intense conversations. She enjoyed watching Kamala and me sing, dance, and laugh together—or at least indulged us—yet would tend to return to encouraging our academic pursuits. And when she spoke, we listened. She was the kind of woman who made you think about what you were going to contribute to the culture at large.

Throughout my younger life, she was another example of a wise, impressive career woman who had carved out her own niche of expertise—namely educating and creating programs within the fields of Black studies and anthropology. She was fervently devoted to creating change and often led efforts within her field to do so. It was empowering that such a woman listened closely to us and took us seriously. She made me feel as if what I was saying was important.

One of my favorite traits about Kamala is her ability to ask clear, direct questions and then genuinely listen to the responses. She has always been the friend who is actually paying attention and listening carefully to what you're saying—a trait due in part, I believe, to the influence of her countless conversations with Aunt Mary.

*   *   *

Aunt Mary and Shyamala shared a mighty bond, one that eschewed bloodlines when it came to deeming others family. Their relationship was similar to what I see between very close real sisters, in that they could tell each other anything, laugh, or have disagreements, but nothing could change the love and respect they had for each other. By extension, Aunt Mary was incredibly close with Kamala and Maya (both of whom she clearly adored) and was very helpful to Shyamala in terms of looking after the girls. A little later, Uncle Sherman and Aunt Mary babysat Meena, Maya's daughter, in her early life. Aunt Mary filled a beautiful role in all their lives, just as they did in hers. Though she was an eminent scholar, activist, film and literary critic, seamstress, and much more, she seemed happiest to me whenever I saw her with her sister Shyamala and with the girls.

Aunt Mary was an essential mentor and key element in the web of brilliant minds who ushered us through our earliest years, influencing and informing us about the world. She was a true auntie for Kamala, an impressive example for all of us, and a steady presence of feminine wisdom and warmth in our community.

Charisma

Robert

The brotherly friendship between my father and Uncle Sherman was the initial, essential connection between our family and this fascinating community of Berkeley activists. But Daddy had a distinct gift for fitting in with anybody, anywhere. When I think back to my childhood, I don't think of him as being entrenched in any movement, or even any particular group of people, so much as I just think of him as being my ever-present father, a man who organized his life around being the ultimate family man—but one whose many friends brought so much color into our home and life.

From my first day of school, he would drop me off and pick me up right out front, without fail. He was very protective of me and of my brother, just as my grandmother was deeply protective of him—as far as Grandma Mary was concerned, the sun rose and set around my dad. It's only with the benefit of hindsight that I've come to understand that their instinct was rooted in a painful family history.

Much of Grandma Mary's (and by extension, my dad's) protective nature was due to the tragic death of his older sister, Bessie Perel. She used to love to carry him around on her hip, bringing him everywhere with her. They were inseparable, until one fateful day when she was crossing a road in Fordyce, Arkansas (where they were born and lived as children), and was struck and instantly killed by a speeding truck. She was twelve years old. The white man who had been driving the truck came by the house later with a sack of potatoes, as if that were how much her life was worth.

Grandma Mary was tough and fiery as can be, and it's no wonder. She gave birth to five children, but after she lost Bessie Perel, my dad was her only surviving child. She'd lost the others at birth or shortly after. She stayed in Arkansas for a few years after Bessie was killed, but soon enough Grandma decided it was time to take my daddy and leave Fordyce behind. In 1942, when Daddy was seven years old, they got on a bus and headed to California to make a fresh new life for themselves in West Oakland. It was just the two of them for a while, though his mother once put Daddy on the Greyhound bus in Oakland to go visit his father in Fordyce. Years later, when sharing the story with us, my father would recall his mama telling her friend, who was on the bus with him, to "look after my son." She told Daddy to stay on the bus the *whole* time, no matter what, and made him promise her not to get off until he reached Fordyce. Daddy did exactly as he was told, so much so that he ended up urinating in his pants to avoid disobeying his mother's instructions.

Back in California, he and Grandma Mary lived together for several years, making do, until his mom met his eventual stepfather, Sam Amey. The family then moved from West Oakland to the Seaport Housing projects in Richmond, California. Even in his early adolescence, my father's sociability flourished; he loved to just hang out at the recreational centers and ball courts in the projects and make friends with everybody. That's where Doris and Robert first met.

Doris was eleven years old; he was twelve. She lived on the border between El Cerrito and Richmond and would often go to the rec centers where Daddy was shooting hoops or chatting with whoever was around. Each noticed the other, but they weren't properly introduced until they met at Richmond's McLaughlin Eastshore State Park, in a clubhouse where Dad often hung around with his friends Don and Eugene. My mom was with two of her best friends, who had planned to meet up with Don and Eugene—leaving Mom and Dad as the awkward third wheels to a double date. She remembers the moment she met the eyes of the cute, shy boy standing there. His hair was very light, almost sandy colored, and he had matching eyelashes. She claims that as soon as their eyes connected, a voice in her head told her, "That is going to be the father of your children."

She listened (though of course she didn't share the premonition). It was clear to both of them that they liked each other, and they started making more intentional plans to meet up at the park. On one occasion he walked her all the way from the Seaport Park projects to her house—roughly three miles away.

As she recalled earlier, she invited my dad and his friends to her twelfth birthday party, but they didn't show up. She was devastated and got very angry, refusing to speak to him for years! The following year, Daddy went to Longfellow Junior High and my mom went to Harry Ells Junior High. Doris held on to her birthday snub grudge for a good while: if she saw him in passing, she would very noticeably pretend that she hadn't and would look the other way.

They both attended El Cerrito High School, but she still didn't speak to him again until her sophomore year (when Dad was a junior). He was sitting a few benches behind her during a student assembly, and she saw him.

"Oh, ain't he cute," she whispered to her best friend, Mittie Ann.

"He sure is," Mittie Ann agreed.

After the assembly they each grabbed one of his hands, teasing and playing a bit of tug-of-war with him.

My mom, now eighty-four years old, still vividly recounts

my dad freely letting go of Mittie Ann's hand but continuing to hold on to hers. They talked for a while, and she agreed to again let him walk her back to her house. At some point she asked him why he hadn't shown up to her twelfth birthday party. He told her he'd never known about it, but she insisted otherwise (and still does, with fervor). At that stage it didn't matter, and that exchange about her party provided a gateway for them to confess to liking each other. So their courting began.

Robert would walk Doris to her classes, even if it meant he'd be late to his own. But one day she noticed him walking another girl, named Jeffreymae, to her classes. She confronted him, but he brushed it off and told her it was nothing. Doris still felt it was disrespectful and—ever inclined to hold somebody accountable for poor behavior—promptly broke up with him.

About a year later was her senior prom. She got herself all dressed up and was waiting anxiously for her date to pick her up. Somehow, my dad had found out that the guy who was supposed to take her was going to stand her up. So when my grandparents opened the door, expecting my mom's date, my dad was standing there instead. He had already graduated and was attending San Francisco State University at the time. My mom gasped with surprise and delight.

She had remained crazy about my dad and was devastated with jealousy over whatever might have been going on between him and Jeffreymae. To this day she gets heated whenever she shares the story! When my father was still alive and they would reminisce about how they had gotten together, without fail she would get fired up with him about it, while Ronny and I just sat there, incredulous, shaking our heads in disbelief that forty or fifty years on she was *still* holding a grudge.

A few weeks after that unexpected prom date, in June 1954, Dad went by Mom's house and told her that he would not be returning to SF State but would instead be joining the United States Air Force. He served from the summer of 1954 to the tail end of 1957, working in tactical hospitals in Alabama and as a medical service specialist in Japan. He also played basketball for the air force. He was awarded the National Defense Service Medal and Good Conduct Medal, but he would never boast about such things. When he returned home, he attended Oakland City College, Laney campus, where he played basketball and received his diploma in industrial drafting and design in 1960. Soon after, he reconnected once again with Doris, his childhood sweetheart, and they were married in 1962.

Daddy worked at the Co-op grocery store in Berkeley. Consumers' Cooperative of Berkeley was established in 1939, in the wake of the Great Depression. It was based in Berkeley, and at its peak it had over 100,000 members, the largest of its kind in North America. Until the early 1960s its only location was 1414 University Avenue, which is where he started work. It expanded to include a hardware store, a day care called the Kiddie Korral, and a credit union. Of course my parents were members, and they did all their grocery shopping there.

Once they had me, Daddy—who had far greater flexibility with his hours—structured his days to make sure he could take care of me. He would work a split shift or take a late lunch in order to pick me up every day from kindergarten and drop me off with my nanny, then he would go back to work. He continued doing this until I became old enough to walk with my St. Joseph's classmates down to the Sheltons', where my brother was attending preschool.

My brother Ronny is seven years younger than I am, so when he started elementary school, I was in eighth grade, making me old enough to look after both of us on the bus to and from school. But Daddy was still protective and wary. The 43 bus would drop us off just around the corner from our home, on Cornell and Hopkins Streets. Sometimes he would be standing in front of the house, just waiting for us to turn the corner onto Stannage. If I ever appeared and Ronny wasn't right beside me, I was in trouble! I can still hear the rare seriousness that would underlie his voice if ever he had to caution me: "I don't *ever* want to see you turn that corner without your brother, do you hear me?" Those were probably the moments when he was hardest on me; he always wanted to make sure I held Ronny's hand when crossing streets and would become very distressed if I didn't keep him close by my side for that short walk home. I paid close attention, as my dad's temper was almost never raised, nor was his voice, so even the slightest rebuke made a big impression.

Daddy worked in the produce department and knew all about fruit and vegetables and respecting the earth. He loved to bring home unusual vegetables and treats for us to try. He believed deeply in the Co-op's values and was proud when it was nationally recognized for its 1970 decision to carry organic products, ban the sale of hazardous pesticides in stores, and establish a community recycling center in Berkeley. Such initiatives were significant advancements that mattered a great deal to the community at the time.

Even more than my dad, my mom and Shyamala hopped on the recycling bandwagon very early on. Kamala and I would crack up at how each of them would fill her car (Mom's a '66 Mustang and Shyamala's a late-model Dodge Dart) to the brim with large bags full of cans, bottles, newspapers, and cardboard. They were both really into it and actively tried to get the community involved.

Daddy loved being a part of it and was very environmentally

conscious. After the Co-op closed, Daddy got our produce from Monterey Market in the Northbrae area of Berkeley, not far from our house. Monterey Market was at the forefront of farmers markets and was considered a leader of the movement to provide natural and sustainable meat, fish, and produce.

Given his affinity for the food and way of life of Japan (whose culture he came to appreciate during time spent serving there), Daddy also enjoyed shopping at the Tokyo Fish Market on San Pablo Avenue, which was within walking distance of my parents' house. He would chat with the workers while buying fresh fish and authentic ingredients for his delicious ramen noodles, the snack he would make to tide us over until dinner. I have beautiful memories of the sight and smell of him chopping up green onions, slicing mushrooms, boiling an egg, and garnishing our bowls with bean sprouts.

Daddy did a lot of the cooking for the family; he made the best red beans and rice, greens, and cornbread I've ever eaten. He took his time, meticulously dicing up fresh garlic and onion, taking great pleasure in the process. He would get started around noon to allow his red beans and greens to simmer slowly all day. I could smell his beans from the sidewalk leading to our house, which always instinctively made me speed up. He happily told me what ingredients he used to make his beans so delicious, but I could never replicate the taste. Daddy didn't have actual recipes, nor would he use exact measurements. I learned to cook like him, to add spices "by hand"—in other words, by smell and palate.

Throughout my childhood, my father insisted on us eating dinner together every evening. This was never optional. My parents, brother, and I had our regular seats at the table. Dinner was always around six—and no matter where my brother and I were, or what we were doing, we had to come home for dinner. I could be shopping at the El Cerrito Plaza or hanging out on Telegraph or Shattuck Avenue with friends, but I always knew when it was getting close to six o'clock that it was time to venture home.

I have a particularly fond memory of one time, when we were older, when Kamala and I were out and about in Berkeley, driving around in my mom's Mustang. If I had driven her back home to Bancroft Way, it would have made me late for dinner, so I just brought her home with me. My dad was happy to make an extra plate for one of my best friends, and he was especially fond of Kamala because of the relationship that she and Maya had with Uncle Sherman and Aunt Mary. He always cared about her and thought of her as a smart, well-grounded niece. He was a phenomenal judge of character and always recognized that Kamala had a good head on her shoulders. I remember a few times when all of us would huddle around our round white midcentury modern kitchen table to eat dinner. The conversation would be lively and natural, just as it always was with my family.

The six o'clock news was usually on in the background, or would have just aired, giving my parents the opportunity to discuss current events, sports, or politics. The dinner table was also where we'd talk about history and issues like racism—especially during the most active years of the Black Panthers. Daddy would reminisce about his time at Merritt College, where he'd met Bobby Seale and Huey P. Newton. My dad had bought a few of Bobby Seale's books directly from him, as well as from Eldridge Cleaver, which he would show us. He had so many stories, so many connections. He liked to ask questions, and Kamala—or any of my friends who had been invited to join us around the table—was encouraged to engage. Discussion usually ended with Daddy making a funny crack about "some fool carrying on."

After dinner, Kamala and I would go to my room to play a few records on my all-in-one AM/FM radio with a built-in turntable. We hung out for a while and listened to Teena Marie, Earth, Wind & Fire, or a Commodores album, then I drove her home.

Daddy loved Berkeley and seemed to know almost everyone in town. Charismatic and gregarious, he was well liked by everybody, a true people person. He was always hip to what was going on—in the community at large, but also with individual people. It was more than just street smarts. He was sharp and observant and always had a good read on people and situations. He'd let you know through a knowing glance or a subtle comment, but never made a big fuss about it.

He was perfectly suited for our neighborhood and the time, where and when people helped and supported one another a lot. Whether we needed a plumber, painter, electrician, or mechanic, Dad had a friend he could call. He was especially familiar with the Black business owners. Like "Big Daddy," who owned Big Daddys Fish House, a beloved hole-in-the-wall restaurant on San Pablo Avenue, in South Berkeley. It had the best fried fish, and it was always a treat to go there, because Big Daddy took the time to talk with every customer, helping cultivate a strong sense of community and neighborly relations. My dad shared that attitude, making them both typical "Berkeley village" figures.

Much like Uncle Sherman, Daddy was happy to talk with anybody and offer advice or stand in as a role model. As a long-ago basketball star, he had often been noted in papers for scoring the most points, delivering the most assists, and making game-winning shots. One of his favorite things to do was to invite his friends over to shoot hoops in our backyard. He did this until well into his sixties. (Charlie Russell—Bill Russell's brother—had been a friend of his since they were kids in West Oakland and would come over to play with him frequently.)

Daddy was a father figure to many of my close friends, and was the coolest uncle for all of my cousins. He took my first cousin Darryl to the US Olympic boxing trials one night, where they watched Muhammad Ali fight (when he was still known as Cassius Clay). Darryl later recalled my dad telling him to pay very close attention to Clay, because he was an extremely good boxer with great potential. Another cousin, Duane, remembered when Uncle Robert bought him a color TV for his dorm at San Francisco State (this was in 1977, when having a color TV was a very big deal)! He balanced being cool with being bighearted, and he offered both traits freely to our whole community.

I learned so much from my father, it's impossible to articulate the scope of all that he imparted simply by the way he carried himself and the way he treated others. He made us laugh with his quick-witted wisecracks, but he was always dropping in some bits of wisdom along the way—not just for me and Ronny, but for my close friends as well, like Kamala and my friends Colette and Cyndi. He would share little bits of knowledge here and there, and often tell us girls that he didn't want us to "ever fall for the 'okey doke'"—in other words, get taken advantage of for being naive; he was reminding us to be sharp and to see things for what they are...and are not. My friends recognized that he was both book- and street-smart. He imparted wisdom and insight to my girlfriends about dealing with boys, then in turn talked to young men about how to respect girls. Again, like his chosen brother, Uncle Sherman, he had a real knack for teaching others, in one way or another. Both men shared their wisdom in a way that made you pause and think about your words and actions.

Daddy used to often quote from a Billie Holiday song: "God bless the child that's got his own." People interpret that in many ways. To him it meant that he wanted me to make my own way and never wanted me borrowing from others. I should work to take care of myself and to have my own. We can't expect anyone to do anything more than what they're capable of doing. We must always have our own.

Or he'd tell me that if I ever loaned money, I should loan only what I could afford to lose. He never wanted me to put myself in a bad situation—and if I did, or made a bad decision, he would say, in a matter-of-fact tone, "I thought you were smarter than that." Those few words were so effective, and they ensured I'd think twice the next time.

Naturally he made comments to lift me up as well. He might be talking to Mom, or Uncle Sherman, and would often offer asides I'd occasionally overhear, like "My daughter is sharp," or "Stacey knows what's happening." He knew I had a good grasp of concepts and would keep me and Ronny motivated simply by saying, "I know you'll take care of business; you're smart." He taught me how to reason with people by listening to their issue, then talking through it. My mom was always feistier—though neither of them ever encouraged physical fighting. Dad always told me to never hit anyone, and never to let anyone put hands on me. He encouraged me and Ronny to trust that the best way to solve a problem or work through conflict was with our brains. All this was delivered as encouragement. He never lectured us—likely because he knew the impact of his words. Just a few effectively communicated everything he wanted us to know.

As far as role models go, my mom was more typical of a person that one might look up to (I certainly did and still do). She was career driven, a rare female engineer who was always very well put together, wore sharp suits to work, and managed to be very active. My father was a different type. He wore a shirt and tie to work at the Co-op and would always look sharp when going out on the town, but his typical daytime wear was a fresh Adidas jogging suit. He exhibited upstanding behavior in his dedication to family values and the way he treated others. He lived out Dr. King's adage to judge people not by the color of their skin, but rather by the content of their character. But he didn't preach, or ever try to put himself forth as some sort of guide. People were naturally drawn to him. He was down-to-earth and accessible and always said things like, "Right on, right on." Given the era, that made him an important, recognizable member of our community, known and loved by many.

*   *   *

Though he had mastery in the kitchen, his favorite room—and the place where he spent much of his time at home—was the den. My mind's eye still places him on the loveseat (another midcentury modern piece) where he would read from his extensive, unique collection of books while a black-and-white movie on AMC played in the background. Somehow, he managed to catch all the NBA and NFL games as well, especially if the Oakland Raiders were playing. One of his best friends, George Atkinson, played for the Raiders and would often come over to watch other games with him. Especially toward the later seventies, my dad had season tickets for the Golden State Warriors and the Raiders. He would usually take Ronny with him, or my mother would join them so she could have fun with George's wife Beverly.

The den was where Daddy kept his books, albums, and stereo equipment. He loved reading and was especially fond of authors like Eldridge Cleaver, Ralph Ellison, and James Baldwin. He would talk to me about his books all the time, but I didn't take it in nearly as much as my son later did. Daddy and Patrick Jr.—who has inherited several of those key books from his collection—would sit and talk about them for hours. But it wasn't purely intellectual. He also loved sitting in the den and just flipping through the almanac or *The Book of Lists*, or he would take the time to read through an encyclopedia. He savored knowledge and would share it freely in conversation.

Naturally he especially wanted his children to share in that love of knowledge. He wanted me to share his passion for books, so he bought me a Reading Pacer machine—a device that trained me to speedread—then sat with me after school when I was in fourth grade as I learned to quickly run my eyes over a page, absorbing what was most important. As much as he tried to impart his own knowledge, he also showed great respect for what I cared about independently. He knew how much I loved animals, so he would bring home rabbits, guinea pigs, hamsters, turtles, and even a rooster he had brought from his friend's mini farm in the Berkeley Hills.

He hoped that my love of all varieties of species would extend to my enjoying his fish tanks with him. During the late seventies, he installed fish tanks in the den. We had a large tank filled with cichlids: convicts, red devils, *Maylandia*, and oscars. There was a smaller hexagonal tank in which he kept his fish Jack Dempsey, who was my favorite to watch. He would follow my finger as I pressed it against the glass and moved around the exterior of the tank. On the weekends I'd help Daddy clean the tanks, which was fun the first few times but soon became a chore, and by the time I was thirteen or fourteen, I wanted to be out with my friends instead. Dad always enjoyed it; he would start blasting his jazz records out of the open windows of the den and leisurely wipe out the tanks in the backyard, perhaps pausing to share a tidbit from the encyclopedia with a friend who may have stopped by the house to chat with him.

Jazz was his other great passion in life, in addition to our family, Berkeley, cooking, and basketball. Daddy was all up in the jazz scene, and had a lot of friends who were well-known jazz musicians, like George Cables, Freddie Hubbard, Dexter Gordon, Donald Byrd, and Eddie Henderson. These musicians would come by our house, and my parents would go out to hear them play at spots like the Keystone Korner, the Black Hawk, the Playboy Club, the Jazz Workshop (where they met Horace Silver and his band), and, years later, Kimball's.

Our neighbors were well accustomed to hearing jazz blaring from his den. On any given day, Dexter Gordon, Coltrane, Miles, Joe Henderson, or Eddie Henderson would be on at high volume throughout the house. Joe and Eddie were unrelated, but both were good friends of my father. Eddie always stopped by whenever he was coming through the Bay Area on a tour or visiting from New York.

As I advanced through my teenage years, I would answer his jazz by blaring my preferred jams, which came from Stevie Wonder's *Innervisions*, Rufus featuring Chaka Khan, or El Gran Combo's *La Universidad de la Salsa*. Come weekends, I would play my records while Dad had his jazz going down the hall! He respected "my" music and would occasionally cut a few dance moves, but he also wanted me to appreciate classic jazz. We overlapped on musicians like Marvin Gaye and Ronnie Laws, both of whom remain among my favorite artists.

Day to day, Daddy arranged his time and engagements to take care of Ronny and me. He never missed a single track meet, basketball game, or school event, and he made a point of telling me how proud he was of me for finishing what I had started. When I was running track, I was never the fastest, but I loved running, so I kept participating every year. He was always proud of me, which by extension made me feel proud of myself. The one exception was when I came in dead last in the 440-yard run. "Stacey," he told me, "you need to stop trying to be cute and put in the work." Even then, he said as much with kind eyes.

He was an encouraging soul, always. Daddy's friends knew him to be caring and thoughtful, the type of guy who always made it a point to call them on holidays and birthdays. Being present and considerate was his natural vibe.

Connectivity

The Sheltons

There are few people who make permanent, lasting impressions on our lives. Most relationships are fleeting—and while a person may feel important while they're an active member of your day-to-day, their influence wanes as soon as they're physically distant. If you're lucky, you'll meet people outside your family who become essential to the formation of your own character. The reliable connections you create with them are secured for a lifetime, regardless of how long it's been since you last spoke to or saw them. That is the nature of my relationship with Kamala. I feel a similar blessed connection to a very special family that was at the core of our childhood experience: the Sheltons.

My family was lucky enough to become a part of their wide circle of friends when Shyamala introduced my mom to Mrs. Regina Shelton (who was always Mrs. Shelton—never Regina—to Kamala, me, and the rest of the children).

Mrs. Shelton was born in 1922, making her fourteen years older than my mom and sixteen years older than Shyamala. She grew up in Louisiana (and would often have delicious, authentic southern food cooking on the stove) and came west to California to work in the shipyards as a young woman.

Her husband, Arthur, was a gentle soul who was always around the house, quietly fixing things around their day care and Learning Center. He worked the grounds and yards of their nursery and home and generally had an affable way about him. Like his wife, he was clearly a beautiful person. Whenever I would see him walking to or from their houses on Bancroft, he always smiled and was kind. But Mrs. Shelton was the matriarch of not just her family but of the whole community—especially from the perspective of the children.

Shyamala met fellow civil rights activist Aubrey LaBrie when she was at UC Berkeley (along with Sherman and Mary). They formed a swift friendship, and Aubrey invited her to meet his family, which included his maternal aunt, Mrs. Shelton. A sincere connection was forged between Mrs. Shelton and Shyamala, and in no time Kamala was attending Mrs. Shelton's day care. Later, while Kamala and I were at Berkwood, Maya went to the Sheltons' day care—which is when they were introduced into my life.

Mrs. Shelton and her family were another crucial pillar holding up the foundation of our childhood. Mrs. Shelton reminded me of my maternal grandmother with her soft, slightly high-pitched voice and loving smile. Also like my grandmother, she never had to raise her voice to discipline; she had a special gift that allowed her to connect with children naturally, and she would gently let us know when we needed to take it down a notch, or share, or take a few breaths. By instinct, and in response to her tender gaze, we all adored and respected Mrs. Shelton and relished our time in her home of nourishment, music, and connectivity.

She loved children and always knew precisely how to make us feel special and safe when we were in her presence. When she recognized the need for a day care, she created it as an extension of her home. It went on to become Shelton's Learning Center, and over time evolved into Shelton's Primary Education Center (SPEC). Her two daughters, Sharon McGaffie and Judy Robinson (who attended the inauguration), worked as teaching instructors and co-owners of the program. Aunt Mary also spent some time as an educational consultant there, bringing to the center her Afrocentric teaching experience at various colleges throughout the Bay Area.

After Kamala's parents separated, Shyamala and the girls moved from their Milvia apartment to a unit directly above the day care. Mrs. Shelton was a nurturing soul to many in the West Berkeley community. But playing that role for Shyamala, Kamala, and Maya made her especially close to them. Having somebody step in to help, and to do so with the loving generosity that defined Mrs. Shelton, meant a great deal to Shyamala, whose family was in India and who was essentially a single mother for most of the girls' lives.

On Sundays Mrs. Shelton would often bring Kamala and Maya along to her church, Oakland's Twenty-Third Avenue Church of God. Shyamala encouraged this, because the girls were being raised in the Black tradition—though they were also being raised to understand and to appreciate Hinduism. Mrs. Shelton's church had an amazing choir, which helped make the services lively, uplifting community events. I never attended services there, and my mother and I only ever went there to attend Mrs. Shelton's funeral, but it is easy to imagine that her church would have an environment similar to the one cultivated in her home: inclusive, filled with music, and representative of a loving God who offered open arms to all.

In my family we weren't religious per se. I went to Sunday school, and I have no qualms about describing myself as a Catholic, as I was raised in that tradition from first grade through college. But my parents weren't the type to drag us to church every Sunday. We would go to enjoy the choir or be present for whatever our souls needed on any given day. Nevertheless, I would characterize myself and my mother as deeply spiritually connected. I suppose another way to phrase it is by saying that if I'm following my inner spirit, I'm doing what I'm supposed to be doing.

Whenever she went to church, Mrs. Shelton brought along her well-loved Bible...the very same one upon which Kamala laid her hand when being sworn into all her major positions. I like to imagine that each time she's done so, she's been lifted back up and encouraged by the love and positive faith that Mrs. Shelton instilled and encouraged when she was a little girl.

During the period when Maya was attending Mrs. Shelton's day care, she and Kamala would occasionally come over to my house. I remember playing in the den, within earshot of my parents, who were both astounded by the assorted facts about Black history that Maya was sharing, when she couldn't have been much older than two or three. She could speak at length about Frederick Douglass, Harriet Tubman, George Washington Carver, and many others. It was deeply important to the Sheltons, and to my parents, that children start learning Black history from as early as two years old. By Doris's recollection, students who went through the Sheltons' were well ahead of the other students by the time they went to public school.

In the early 1970s, when Ronny was two years old, my parents were eager to sign him up for their day care nursery. Unfortunately, the class was completely full. My mom talked to Shyamala, who kindly beseeched Mrs. Shelton to make an exception and squeeze one more child in. My parents were so grateful to both Shyamala for the nudge and Mrs. Shelton for agreeing to accept him, as they recognized the phenomenal value of the educational experience and environment provided there. He went on to attend their Learning Center classes as well as kindergarten. Ronny well remembers his experience at the Learning Center due to the warmth of its family atmosphere and sense of community. In retrospect, having been there makes him feel as if he was "part of a movement." I too remain forever grateful to Shyamala for making sure that happened, as Ronny going there was what enabled us all to remain connected to the extended family and web of support provided by the Sheltons and their inviting backyard.

During Ronny's time there, my mother developed a close relationship with Mrs. Shelton as well as with her daughters, Judy and Sharon. My mom always appreciated the way the Sheltons treated not just the children, but also the parents, like family. She loved taking us to the pancake breakfasts they would host—which Shyamala, Kamala, and Maya would always be a part of—or to the roller skating parties they would organize. The Sheltons' facilities and leadership connected the generations as well as the children, further enforcing the sense that we were being raised by many hands.

With my brother and Maya attending the day care and Kamala and me at elementary schools in Berkeley, their home was the most natural place to convene after school while we waited for our mothers to get off work. Older siblings looked after younger ones, and we were all encouraged to take care of one another—all under the loving eyes of Mrs. Shelton.

St. Joseph's was within walking distance, so after school I'd head toward their houses on Bancroft Way, usually with Carole and other kids in our class who lived near the Sheltons. Kamala was still being bused to and from Thousand Oaks Elementary School, but at the end of the school day, she would be dropped off a block away from the Sheltons' houses. They came to own three on the same block on Bancroft Way: their family home, a two-story home with the downstairs converted into the day care and an apartment unit on top, and the Learning Center, which sits on the corner of Bancroft Way and Curtis.

The three locations being so close made it convenient for us children to roam freely, whether we were hanging out in the main house or walking to the day care and Learning Center to check on our younger siblings. Sometimes we would help pass out juice and snacks to the younger children, who would often be waking up from their afternoon nap. Kamala, some of the other older kids, and I would usually play out back on the swings and slides at the Learning Center.

It was a welcoming, respectful environment that nurtured us. And there was always fun to be had at the Sheltons'. The yard buzzed with activity and consistent sounds of children laughing, learning, and playing together. Mrs. Shelton usually would have Motown music playing from the house as we ran around the yard.

On the walls were posters of Sojourner Truth, Harriet Tubman, and several other important historical Black figures. Those posters were all around the school, featured to inspire curiosity, awareness, and a sense of profound pride. Mrs. Shelton delighted in sharing stories and discussing these leaders with anybody who asked.

When our mothers arrived from work to pick us up, there was never any hurry to get us out of there or rush us home. They would mingle for a while, talking and laughing themselves, before each group headed home for dinner. I give endless tribute to Mrs. Shelton and her family for creating such an active, loving community for children and for their mothers (in particular). She built a foundation of inclusive goodness that was both an environment and an education in how to behave, namely how to treat every person with decency and respect. Her gentle nature was given out indiscriminately, especially when it came to kids. She engaged with all the children as if they were her own and made sure each one of us felt special.

Kamala has a natural gift with children—she demonstrated it with my own kids, and I've watched her engage with young people in a similar manner throughout her career and on her campaign trails. She always had that instinct with Maya, of course, but I trust that a great deal of the nurturing of that instinct happened at the Sheltons'. As a politician, Kamala has exhibited a fierce determination to protect women and children. One assumes much of that is drawn from her own childhood and being raised by a single mother. But when I see such advocacy, I also think of Mrs. Shelton and the great emphasis she put on childcare and on helping mothers balance a successful career and a supported family life.

Though every child who entered that home would immediately feel heard and important, Kamala and Maya likely were even more at home, given the relationship between Shyamala and the Sheltons and the fact that they lived just above the day care. But Mrs. Shelton treated every child as family.

When I got older and had children of my own, I developed an even more profound understanding of and sense of wonder and awe at what a blessing she was—for Shyamala, of course, but also for my mom and for the many other working women who were doing their best to raise young children while maintaining careers. When we were at the Sheltons', our mothers didn't need to give a second thought to whether or not their children were in a secure, nurturing environment. During the day, and often into the evening, she eliminated that concern for scores of parents.

Thanks to Mrs. Shelton's influence, and to my parents, and

to the colorful network of support from my friends and from the adults around us, I had the rare experience of truly loving my childhood. I even had positive experiences at each of the schools I attended. When I had my two children, it was important to me to give them similarly wonderful roots—not only in education but also in terms of a sense of community. I wanted them to be in an environment where they could learn to socialize well, develop diverse friendships, and always feel valued and included.

I knew precisely where to start. My daughter, Lauren, and son, Patrick, are four years apart, and both of them attended the Sheltons' day care and Learning Center. As my mother did with me, I picked each of them up after work, which meant that, also like my mother, I could focus on my work during the day with the peace of mind of knowing that my children were being exquisitely well cared for.

By that time it was the 1990s, and Shelton's Learning Center had expanded to Shelton's Primary Education Center and grown from the two houses on Bancroft Way to a larger campus near the Elmwood area of Oakland. The school held classes for day care through fifth grade. In addition to the standard curriculum, it offered a variety of African history, art, music, and dance classes.

Though the school was significantly larger, the environment had retained the warmth, active energy, focus on freedom of expression, and cultural pride instilled by Mrs.

Shelton. Young Lauren would come home having learned a few phrases in Swahili as well as West African greeting songs, which she performed with her dance class. I felt a wonder similar to what my parents must have felt when they heard Maya discussing Black history as a toddler.

Lauren still has fond, vivid memories of those African dance classes and of students and professional musicians coming into classes and playing the drums and singing. Just as I did, she loved the energy of being outside on the swings in the Sheltons' yard, drinking Capri Suns with her friends. Watching Lauren dance and sing "Funga Alafia, Ashe Ashe," (an expression of peace, friendship, and welcoming) onstage at age five, I was imbued with gratitude that she was being taught to love and appreciate who she was and where she had come from—and that soon my son would be too. That's what the Sheltons were all about. Providing good education, filling the children's lives with art and music, and instilling Black pride within the comfort of a safe family environment.

Starting from its connection with our mothers, throughout the years of my upbringing, and on down to my children, the Shelton family is a marvelous, blessed thread winding through three generations, tightening bonds along the way, always acting as a connecting force and a source of great comfort. The ability to connect disparate people and to make them feel welcome, make them feel heard, and make them feel as if they belong is another characteristic I see in Kamala, one that brings me back to Mrs. Shelton and how she united us. My gratitude runs deep for the priority she placed on inclusivity and childcare for our Berkeley community. Her influence has continued; her legacy lives on.

Engagement

Adapting

It wasn't until I was in middle school that I started to appreciate the diversity and progressive environment Kamala and I had grown up believing to be normal. My parents had always had close friends of various races and religions, whereas most of my cousins living in Stockton, San Francisco, and other cities had grown up almost exclusively with Black kids, plus maybe a handful of Hispanic families that lived in their neighborhoods.

When I was a kid, there was a constant flow of multiethnic activity and activists around me. And children were rarely excluded or kept sheltered from our simultaneously widespread and tight-knit community of engaged, civic-minded people. I never had a sense that I didn't belong amid the action or that I was too young to understand (though, naturally, I was).

My mom taught me—by example—that we should always

be fighting for justice, but that didn't necessarily mean constantly protesting and taking part in demonstrations. She rarely participated in such gatherings, because she had to prioritize going into the city and working. But she was always involved in some sort of drive, always ready to donate or lend a hand. In addition to her work with Las Electras, Mom was an advocate for the SNCC (Student Nonviolent Coordinating Committee) and supported the Southern Christian Leadership Conference (SCLC), of which Martin Luther King Jr. was a member. She had actually seen him speak, in 1961, and even shook his hand. She and my grandmother had gone to the Progressive Baptist Church on Alcatraz Avenue in Berkeley to see Dr. King as he was going around the country, raising funds, speaking to the masses, and educating people. It was standing room only, but she found a seat for her mother, then stood in the back to listen to him speak and explain the Civil Rights Movement. Before and after and up to this day, she has always supported efforts that contribute to equality and advancement for Black people.

Doris never hesitates to challenge an injustice, whether by writing letters, petitioning, or donating funds. To this day, even if it's a seemingly insignificant incident—it could be as minor as the ignorance of a salesperson at a department store—if she feels she's been wronged, she will write a letter. She's always been insistent that matters should be taken care of in the right way, the proper way. If they're not, it's our responsibility to speak up.

Beyond my parents' lessons, I knew (with a gradual, accruing sense of awareness) that I was growing up in a culture of engaged citizens who were trying to create change for the greater good. That was the nature of Berkeley's influence. Kamala and I were raised among people who, if they saw injustice, determined that it was their responsibility to do something about it. This culture extended beyond core pillars who were like family, but these figures and their examples were no less inspiring.

One of my parents' closest friends, Maylou Bartlett, was very engaged in the community and did a lot of inventive activism. She made a point of getting involved in improving the city's racial politics. Maylou had gotten her teacher's degree from UC Berkeley in the late 1960s. Always active in protests, she was initially a member of CORE (Congress of Racial Equality), but because, unfortunately, there was a consequential stigma surrounding CORE and she did not want anything on her record to prevent her from teaching, she then became an advocate (rather than a member, which required a deeper involvement).

My dad first met Maylou and Jim (her lifelong partner and father of her children) at the Co-op on University Avenue. They became quick friends, and Daddy started taking me over to their house to visit when I was a young girl. Maylou would give me paper and fresh crayons to draw with while I was there, to keep me entertained while they discussed Berkeley and what was happening in the city.

In the sixties and seventies, Maylou—who is white and Jewish—would go into a bank (or several) with a Black man to request a loan. Then she'd go back a couple of days later with a white man, be treated completely differently, and advertise the unjust discrepancy as a means of protest. It was a kind of practical activism. These good friends of my parents were instrumental in the change that occurred in Berkeley over the decades. Maylou remains one of my mom's best friends and is still whip smart, caring, considerate, and involved. (Much later, when I began fundraising efforts for Kamala's presidential campaign, she and my mom were the first to donate to the cause.)

Though all kinds of activity was swirling around the city, our neighborhood was rather calm and inclusive, in the best possible way. It was very culturally diverse, with tons of kids around with whom we played outside nearly every day. All the families knew one another and chatted as we ran around—there was the Louie family next door (Chinese); the Perez family across the street (with a German mom and a Mexican dad); the Poseys (Black); the Haradas (Japanese), and our beloved friends Gladys and Mary, sisters who bought houses across the street from each other on the corner of Stannage Avenue. Such variety was among the gifts of growing up in Berkeley—and is a testament to the town. It helped that my parents, especially Dad, knew and had solid relationships with seemingly everyone in the neighborhood (and the city).

One character who was good friends with Dad was Johnny Apperson. Johnny came to our house often, and I would listen to him and my parents talking about the political climate of the city and beyond. Johnny eventually went to DC to work for Ron Dellums when he became Congressman Dellums. Dellums was a vocally antiwar, openly socialist Democrat who was persuaded by the community to run for city council. Within a few years, he was elected to Congress, and he served there for almost three decades.

Whenever Johnny came home, he would make sure to stop by our house to check in with my dad and keep him abreast of what was going on in DC. Those conversations would spill into our family meals, as—to their credit—my parents were eager for me and Ronny to understand not just Berkeley but the country at large.

Also connected to Dellums was a woman named Maudelle Shirek, who worked at the credit union of the Co-op when my dad was also working there. Like Daddy, she was from Arkansas, and she was always friendly and outgoing, full of life and genuinely concerned about the well-being of the community, particularly its elders. She was also enormously influential in Berkeley politics and had been among those who actively, relentlessly encouraged Dellums to run for Berkeley city council. Years later, she herself ran, at the age of seventy-one. More than two decades later, at the ripe age of ninety-two, she decided to retire as city councilwoman, as the oldest publicly elected official in the United States at the time.

Back when people like Maudelle and Johnny had finally convinced Dellums to run, my mom's friend Hynethia—a very colorful, articulate, Afrocentric woman—had worked as an active member of his campaign committee. I was friends with Hynethia's daughter, Anita, who attended Berkwood and was in the same class as me and Kamala. My mom volunteered to help Hynethia with local canvassing and making sure that people were getting out to vote.

I always loved to accompany my mom to Hynethia's vibrant home, where they discussed the campaign and rallies and got very animated about how best to get people registered and spread the word. Whereas Kamala had been explicitly included in protests from a very young age, my own sense of political activism and justice was nurtured more gradually, through exposure to people like Maylou, Johnny, Maudelle, and Hynethia. Either way, the imprint was left on all of us at that time. That was a consistent takeaway of my childhood and adolescence: if we expect to see any change in our world,

My mom, Doris Bradley, with her homeroom class at El Cerrito High School in 1952.

Boosters

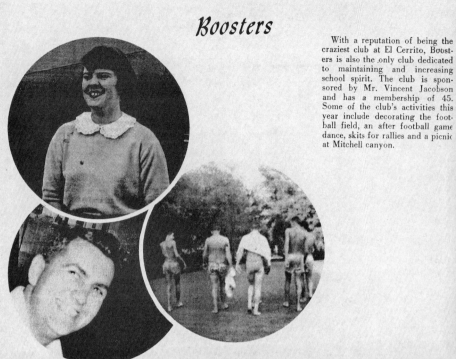

With a reputation of being the craziest club at El Cerrito, Boosters is also the only club dedicated to maintaining and increasing school spirit. The club is sponsored by Mr. Vincent Jacobson and has a membership of 45. Some of the club's activities this year include decorating the football field, an after football game dance, skits for rallies and a picnic at Mitchell canyon.

Mom has always been engaged and full of spirit!

Held for the first time in the school's history was *"Government Day."* During the *"Day"* the presidents and secretaries of six eastbay schools studied El Cerrito's legislature, judicial and executive departments and also explained their governmental systems. The schools attending were San Lorenzo, Richmond, Albany, McClymonds, Fremont, and Alameda. It is hoped that this will become an annual event on the school calendar.

Held for the first time in the school's history was Government Day. Presidents and secretaries of six East Bay schools studied El Cerrito's legislature, judicial, and executive departments.

Officers Fall 1952

MARCIA MARCOS
Secretary

GARY GINDER
President

DAVID JONES
Vice President

PRESIDENT'S MESSAGE

I would like to express my sincere thanks to the faculty and student body of El Cerrito High School for their support during my term as Student Body President.

I think that the past semester has been both eventful and successful. Our student body enrollment has grown tremendously and our enthusiasm, spirit, and traditions have grown proportionally. *"Hello Day"* and *"Homecoming"* are traditions which have been established and which, I am sure, will be long lived.

I have truly enjoyed my term of office; it has been a very memorable experience. To my successor I wish the best of everything.

GARY GINDER

MARILYN COULTER
Commissioner of Finance

LEE GUSTAFSON
Commissioner of Athletics

JOYCE BUCCIARELLI
Commissioner of Entertainmen

DORIS
BRADLEY

NANCY
LEWIS

MARGIE
HAMMERICKSEN

ELINOR
EMELDI

JO ANN
WINTER

JOYCE
JOHNSO

My mom was the first Black Yell Leader at El Cerrito High School in 1952.

My mom sitting at her desk at Pacific Bell as an engineering aid, her position before being promoted to an engineer manager in the early 1960s.

This is one of my favorite pictures of my parents. They were visiting Carlos, one of my dad's best friends in Seattle, 1966.

Mom and Dad with Dad's friend Van Lewis and a member of Horace Silver's band circa 1959. Mom's friend Marion held a party for the band at her house. They were quite the socialites!

Kamala wearing the green jumper and me with two ponytails behind her. Berkwood kindergarten field trip circa 1969.

Kamala's birthday party, "Will someone please light the candles!" circa 1969.

My mom and my little brother, Ronny. Mom and I loved our Afros in the early 1970s.

Maya, Shyamala, Kamala, and Meena attending my wedding. St. Joseph's Church in Berkeley, September 10, 1988.

Good times at 1555 Lakeside Drive in Oakland as first-time home buyers!

Mother's Day brunch held at Kamala's condo in the mid-1990s. Mom and Shyamala always enjoyed their time together.

"Aunt" Mary enjoying the Mother's Day brunch.

Precious moments: Kamala attentive to my son, Patrick, during our Mother's Day brunch. Patrick Jr. was around four years old in this picture.

Quick "photo op" at my sister-in-law Ingrid Jane's wedding at the Grace Cathedral in San Francisco, May 1996.

This was taken at a baby shower my sister-in-law Ingrid gave for me when I was pregnant with my son in 1991.

This is my father's longtime good friend George Cables, jazz composer and piano legend. Yoshi's in San Francisco, June 2019.

Mom and me with another one of my dad's very best friends, world-renowned trumpeter Eddie Henderson. Taken after he and George's performance at Yoshi's.

A very special evening when Kamala came for ISCLA's performance of *The Two Gentlemen of Verona*. Griffith Park Shakespeare Festival.

Mom and me with Judy Shelton Robinson and Sharon Shelton McGaffie at a fundraiser in Oakland for Kamala's presidential campaign.

"Friends from the Beginning"

everyone needs to find a way to do their part, without ever letting up.

———————

All these lessons that had been embedded in me from growing up in Berkeley left their mark and were invaluable lived examples. But Berkeley was also just a great place to come of age, as it offered a great sense of the larger world beyond it. As we grew up, weekends were spent lingering on University, Bancroft, Telegraph, and Shattuck Avenues—the active thoroughfares that lead straight to Cal from all local freeways—which introduced us to new communities, like the Hare Krishna, who played tambourines and chanted in light-colored, flowy garments.

Telegraph Avenue, probably the most popular among them, ending near the entrance to Sproul Plaza on Bancroft Way, was always packed on weekends. At any turn you were likely to catch a whiff of an unusual smell, whether incense or marijuana. The street was lined with T-shirt print shops, shoe stores, and record stores (such as Tower Records right off Telegraph, on Durant), where we'd frequently go to peruse the latest albums. We'd pass by countless international cafés, the ever-busy Blondie's Pizza, and all sorts of vendors with stalls all along the sidewalk, selling absolutely everything you don't need, from handmade jewelry to kufi caps, body oils, tie-dyed T-shirts, and buttons heralding peace. I loved buying those little tokens from Telegraph that I could button onto my school backpack and uniform sweater pockets. I had way more buttons than anybody would ever need—some with slogans on them, others with band names or cute little sayings, but the dominant decorations I went for were those yellow smiley faces and peace signs.

None of this made me feel like we were part of a radical generation, or growing up in its wake, or in the midst of what some would call an ongoing revolution against "the man." Such activity, and all the paraphernalia born from it, were just the norm—those were the sights, smells, and sounds of our weekends, and they provided full and festive afternoons that carried me and my peers throughout my childhood and into our teenage years.

For high school I went to Presentation High School, in Berkeley. It was an all-girls Catholic school with sister locations in San Francisco and Los Angeles. Our Berkeley location was established in 1878 and closed in 1988, soon after Saint Mary's College High School, one of our all-boys "brother" schools, became coed. My former husband, Patrick Batiste, went to Saint Mary's, as did my daughter and son.

Kamala was still in Montreal throughout high school, but we remained in touch, and I can still trace the influence that she had on my life. One memory that demonstrates that to me is of a little confrontation I had when I was in ninth grade. One of my classmates had stolen the jacket to my navy jogging suit that Daddy had just bought for me to wear before and after track practice. I saw a flash of it when she opened her locker and recognized it as mine. She was taller and bigger than I was, and had a reputation for not being the nicest girl in school. But I couldn't go home without my new jacket. As much as I hated the thought of a fight, I needed to get it back. I thought of how Kamala always stood up to bullies and never let anyone—even a five-year-old—get away with misbehavior. The notion of confronting this classmate was extremely uncomfortable for me, but I thought through how to handle it and toughened myself up. I approached her privately and asked her to give it back, because my dad had just bought me the suit and it meant a lot to me. I told her that I would get in trouble if I went home without it and that I didn't want to create a scene or embarrass either one of us. I promised that I wasn't going to say anything to anybody else but said that she needed to hand it over to me. She stared at me, and I just stared right back at her, looking up and not letting my eyes stray. To my utter shock, she finally shrugged, reached into her locker, and handed it back to me! It was a small victory, naturally, but it was one of those moments that bolstered my confidence in myself and in speaking plainly to make things right. This classmate and I didn't run in the same circles, but after that episode, we gained mutual respect for each other, and we even became friendly. I walked away from the situation feeling as if I could negotiate just about anything.

Girls who went to Presentation and to Holy Names in Oakland were invited to run for homecoming queen. Perhaps following in the ambitious tradition of my mother (the first Black cheerleader at her high school), I decided as a sophomore that I might as well give it a go and run for St. Mary's homecoming queen. The process was an intimidating one, but one that led to my first encounter with true love.

It was the initial interview night for those in the running. I sat waiting in a classroom at St. Mary's, looking around at my competition with a growing sense of dread. I was out of my league. All the other girls were older, wore makeup, and seemed far more glamorous than I did. I sucked in my lips anxiously, taking note of all the girls wearing bold red lipstick, in comparison to the gloss I had on.

The process (even at the time, but far more so in retrospect) was bizarre. All the girls filed out so that a panel of boys—our peers!—from various grades could interview us one by one. I smiled nervously at my friend Robert Gardner, a comforting face, who had been my classmate at St. Joseph's. Sitting near him was a boy named Patrick Batiste. Patrick kept staring at me, smiling. My nerves were on full display as I tried hard not to stutter during every response. I was wearing a purple dress with red circles on it, made from the kind of silk that reveals any amount of moisture. I sensed sweat rings forming under my armpits and clamped my arms down anxiously. But the more I tried to hide the sweat, the more I could feel my armpits dripping. All the while, Patrick just kept his eyes on me, smiling.

We continued to see each other at high school dances and parties. I was friends with his cousins, one of whom, Joseph Edgerly Jr. (Joey), often said later that he'd been sure since high school that one of his cousins would marry me. Some of my classmates had gone to Saint Jerome Catholic School with Patrick (for elementary) and had crushes on him. He seemed sweet, but we didn't get together immediately.

The Presentation class of 1982 has remained in remarkably close contact to this day, nearly four decades later. More than twenty of us are on a group text thread that is active almost every day with life news or general commentary. Our friend Carole is the de facto leader and organizer for the crew, and the text thread has proven an amazing means of keeping in touch about significant events that have happened to one of us or to someone we all know from Berkeley. (Needless to say, my phone was constantly abuzz throughout the 2020 runoffs and election—and during most of Kamala's major campaigns over the years.)

My senior year at Presentation, I was accepted to the three universities to which I'd applied: UC Davis, UC Santa Cruz, and UC Berkeley. I have always loved animals, and at the time my dream was to become a veterinarian—which was the thinking behind my application to Davis. Similarly, I'd envisioned working with the dolphins and orcas, which is what inspired my application to the spectacular marine biology program at UC Santa Cruz. My dad and Uncle Sherman had insisted that I apply to UC Berkeley as well.

Much to their disappointment, I eventually decided to enroll in Davis's animal science program—and once I'd made up my mind, I could not wait to attend. My acceptance was contingent upon my attending Davis's Special Transitional Enrichment Program, designed to help acclimate high schoolers to the rigors of college life and academics.

UC Davis introduced me to a great number of things—including segregation. Other than the very rare occasion (like the time, during a family road trip out of state, when we were not seated and were ignored due to being Black), I had never endured an awareness of "otherness" and the differing treatment that came along with that. College changed that. I had grown up in a community that celebrated Black pride. It was all around me, from the paintings and statues displayed in my parents' house to discussions of the Back-to-Africa Movement and the Black Panthers (whose breakfast program was, at one point, held at West Campus on University Avenue, where I went to take summer swimming lessons). My parents and their friends made sure I knew who and what I was, so it's not as if I were not racially conscious. But our community also taught me, explicitly and also by the nature of my diverse city, to embrace everyone, no matter the color of their skin.

There was a period in the 1970s when my mom and I both loved to wear our hair in big Afros. My mom, the fashion designer and seamstress, made matching dashiki shirts for herself and my dad. They wore African jewelry given to them by their friend Ted Pontiflet, who regularly traveled to the continent. We occasionally went to a restaurant in San Francisco called the Beginning, which was owned by Nate Thurmond and featured soul food and African-inspired dishes. It was around this time, in the late seventies, that Daddy switched us from eating meat. Our heritage was a source of intrigue, and I suppose I was among the lucky ones for whom growing up in an unsheltered environment, such as Berkeley's, ironically meant shelter from the divisions and segregated realities of the country at large.

In Berkeley my parents and their friends supported whatever movement was going on to lift up all people, with particular emphasis on making sure Black people were well educated and encouraged to advance. When I left home, I encountered very different perspectives about color and race. Only then did I realize that I would not only be perceived as an outsider but also be categorized differently because of it.

This became obvious from the moment we were assigned

to our dormitories. I was placed in one called Hughes Beckett, or "Beckett" as some called it. The dorm building was intended almost entirely for Blacks, Hispanics, Native Americans, and other underrepresented students. I did notice that it was a little strange that all those who weren't white were placed in a different building, but it didn't really bother any of us at the time, because we were sharing the experience. As a way of claiming it, we cracked jokes, referring to Beckett as "the projects" and laughing about it.

Looking back, decades later, I wonder if the separation or concentration of "like" groups was a benefit or a hindrance. Maybe it was better for us to share a space; perhaps it fostered a sense of solidarity. Still, it seems like a strange decision by the college to establish those divisions. It was my nature to make friends and to date guys of other ethnicities, and being assigned to Beckett didn't get in the way of my meeting people around campus and in my classes. Today, as we continue to reckon with the aftermath of the Black Lives Matter protests, and as Black, brown, and Asian communities continue to be treated as if they all belong in a different building from the white population, it's harder to just laugh about our being placed in "the projects," and I'm left questioning the intent, the message, and the long-term effects of separating the races in such a manner. Whom was it really for? Were we being protected, or were the white kids being protected from us? But again, at the time, we accepted it and just had fun.

*   *   *

Kamala's college experience was vastly different from mine. She had always been set on going to a historically Black college or university (HBCU), and she wanted it to be Howard University. It was a desire long held that she turned into a reality. That's all I heard her talk about: Howard. Her mind was made up, and that was that. My mother had very much wanted me to attend an HBCU, even if only for a semester or a year. She proposed that I apply or look into attending Howard with Kamala and share in that very special experience. At the time, being only nineteen years old and having just made new friends, I couldn't imagine uprooting myself and moving from UC Davis to go to DC for just one semester, much as I missed my friend.

Kamala and I wrote to each other while we were in college. I remember one of the first letters she sent, which had Snoopy on the front of it. Inside she wrote that all the people she was meeting at Howard were nice and interesting, she gave me the number of the pay phone outside her dorm, and she closed out by saying, "I sure hope when you write me, you're writing me from UC Davis and not UC Berkeley," or something to that effect. We knew the pressure we had both received from Uncle Sherman and my dad, and each just wanted the other to be happy wherever she was.

We called each other when we got the chance, especially if we had really big news to share (big news being a new boy we liked, or something of that urgent variety), but long distance was expensive, particularly on pay phones. Hers was directly outside her dorm room, and my roommate and I had one in our dorm room so it was convenient to call, as long as we had saved up enough coins. Kamala was loving her education and getting out of it everything it had to offer, both academically and socially. We kept on our paths and immersed ourselves in our college experiences.

After two and a half years, it became clear that I had perhaps chosen the wrong career path. I was spending a lot of my time in the animal science labs, and I adore animals... arguably too much for that kind of role. Considering that I cry anytime I see an animal get hurt, abused, or apparently injured, I determined that what I'd thought was my dream job was bound to take an emotional toll. I tried to amend that by narrowing it down, and I just worked with agricultural animals for a while. I loved learning about cows, sheep, and horses, and the program enabled us to be around them. We got to shear sheep, check their teeth, all those little things that keep them healthy. We milked the cows and learned about their stomachs and anatomy—and I was fine with all that. But then it came time to do a whole lot of dissecting. I was just like, "*Oh, oh, oh,* how can I *do* this?"

The breaking point with me was likely when I was carrying around a petri dish with cats' eyes in it. Looking down,

I finally thought, "Oh Jesus. I'm done, I'm done." It was too hard for me! Turns out that holding a deep reverence for every living thing didn't work so well when it came to a career as a veterinarian—though I have the utmost respect for those who can handle it! It just wasn't for me.

So I went home. My father opened his arms to me, but was also like, "See, you should've listened to Daddy!" He had fought so hard against my decision to go to Davis, but I had been adamant. Again, he and Sherman had been vehemently opposed, and almost baffled, by my and Kamala's respective decisions. Through their eyes UC Berkeley was the best university in the world, and since I had gotten accepted there, there was simply no good reason *not* to attend. My mom stayed neutral and told me that I should do whatever would make me happy and go wherever I thought I would succeed the most. I probably should have listened to my dad and Uncle Sherman's advice and taken that route...but I have no regrets.

Before we knew it, Kamala and I were both back home in the Bay Area. Kamala had graduated from Howard and loved her experience there. During her last year she had become a member of Alpha Kappa Alpha, the nation's oldest Black sorority, which she spoke of with great pride. She was also part of the debate team, which launched her into her next institution: Hastings Law School in San Francisco—following

Uncle Sherman's avid encouragement that we should all get law degrees, even if we didn't intend on being lawyers. He always told us that knowing the law would be useful and that understanding our rights would mean we would always be able to take care of ourselves.

I started working as a cocktail waitress and bartender at a hot spot called Carlos Murphy's in Emeryville, which no longer exists. Back in the eighties it was wildly popular and very much the place to be. I was there for a year and a half and had a great time, but I soon found myself burned out on that kind of work. My mom sat me down and said, "Look, until you figure out what it is you want to do, you can come work for Pacific Bell."

"Aw, thanks, Mom…but no," I told her. "I don't want to do that." Always one to make things happen, she just gave me *that* look. "Hmm. Well, I got you set up to come on board temporarily as an 'O' operator to work strike duty with me. You might be able to get on permanently as an operator at the phone company, and in the meantime you can make some extra money, have benefits, and figure things out."

I've always been fairly quick with technology, so, without ever really having the intention of following in my mom's footsteps, I said, "OK, fine," and began working for Pacific Bell.

Though we'd initially just maintained a friendship, I had started dating Patrick—the boy who had kept smiling at me throughout the homecoming audition. Our relationship had begun around 1985, when I had returned home from UC Davis. He and his cousin Joey had come to visit a few times while I was at Davis, and he was attending Sacramento City College. We started dating seriously once I got home, and while I was working in downtown Oakland as an operator, I got pregnant.

During my pregnancy I had a dream about our daughter and saw her vividly, looking precisely like the baby she would soon become. My beautiful daughter, Lauren, was born on February 17, 1987. Patrick and I weren't married at the time, but I genuinely didn't feel the need to pressure him about it. I was thrilled at the thought of becoming a mom and saw it as meant to be. My parents didn't feel *exactly* the same way about the situation, or at least not at first. But they soon came around and started pampering me, making sure I was eating the right food and getting enough rest. I was already on top of it and became pretty much vegetarian during my pregnancy.

"What is *he* going to do?" My father would ask, employing the stern voice that I so rarely heard from him. It didn't matter to me: I was set on having our baby and was excited. Despite my father's initial reservations about Patrick and his intentions, the two of them actually got along very well. They both loved jazz (although Patrick's always been more of a contemporary jazz fan, favoring the likes of Jean-Luc Ponty,

Jeff Lorber, and George Duke). They were also both big Raiders fans and would attend games together.

My closest girlfriends—Kamala included—were incredibly supportive, which helped enhance and maintain my own excitement. They were amazed; I was the first in our group to have a baby. That made Lauren extra special—in a sense she was our whole group's first baby! They all checked in on me throughout my pregnancy, ensuring that I never felt alone in the process.

Patrick and I got married on September 10, 1988, a year and a half after Lauren was born. Baby Lauren walked down the aisle as our flower girl. We had a big, boisterous wedding with a guest list that started at 150 but then just kept growing. As we neared the big day, my parents' phone rang off the hook with people asking if they could be added to the list. It got out of hand, with far more people coming than my mom's budget allowed. Patrick and I were both popular locally, with large families and all kinds of acquaintances who wanted to be "on the scene." When I look back, flipping through our two thick wedding albums, there are plenty of people I don't recognize at all, and several others who had absolutely no business being there! Of course, at the time I didn't mind at all.

To this day I smile and marvel at the humongous shoulders on my wedding dress and my bridesmaids' dresses. They were big enough to take out a linebacker! We did it all: ice sculpture with large shrimp placed around it, champagne fountain flowing all night at our party at the Officer's Club on Yerba Buena island. Kamala looked fabulous in a white suit. And of course Shyamala, Maya, and even Maya's daughter Meena were all there to help celebrate that significant turning point in my life journey. I had an amazing time and was on the dance floor for most of the night. But Doris chatted with the three of them for a while at the reception. After most of the guests had eaten dinner, some small groups formed in the bar's lounge area, where there were couches. Mom made a point of walking to each table to greet everyone, and she lingered for a while to sit down with Kamala, Maya, and Shyamala, who were sitting together. Little Meena was enjoying herself as one of the four small children at the wedding (including my daughter, Lauren, who was eighteen months at the time). Doris and Shyamala caught up, spoke about what a beautiful wedding it had been, and laughed as they watched their granddaughters bop around me on the dance floor.

Joy

The Lake

A year or two into our marriage, Patrick, Lauren, and I moved to a two-bedroom apartment in Oakland, on Lakeshore Avenue. We lived directly across from Oakland's Lake Merritt, a location as lovely as it was convenient. Lucky's, Thrifty's, and Merritt Bakery were a stone's throw away. I jogged (or sometimes laced up my white leather roller skates with yellow wheels and gold pom-poms and skated) around the lake—which is just over three miles around—whenever I got the chance. Over time, several of our friends and cousins got apartments nearby, which made the regular weekend concerts and the annual Festival at the Lake local, lively events and gathering points. Around that time downtown Oakland had been transformed into a real hot spot for jobs, restaurants, bars, and nightclubs—and all were easy to stroll to and from. The lake, which sits just east of all that, was the place to be!

Kamala bought her first property soon after, in the early nineties. It was a fabulous condo on Lakeside Drive, within sight of the Alameda County Court House. She loved her place and encouraged me to buy one in the same building. "I would love to, but you know there's no way Patrick and I could afford that!" I told her. We were in our early thirties, and Patrick and I were struggling to cover our rent each month, plus we had to keep up with Lauren's tuition at the Sheltons' SPEC, and we were both still figuring out our job situations. I was starting to move up the ranks at Pacific Bell and was surprised to find that I actually enjoyed the work. Patrick was working with his uncle Joseph at his termite and pest control company, along with three of his cousins. We didn't have much to speak of by way of savings, and I was sure that our money was just too tight for us to make such a big move. Buying a home seemed like something that would have to wait.

But Kamala had planted the seed, and I couldn't stop thinking about the possibility. She put me in touch with her Realtor and friend, Bill Hangston, and suggested I just give him a call to figure out what it would take for my little family to get our first home there. I did so, and with the generous help of my mother and my father-in-law, we were able to pull together and secure the down payment. I was over the moon about the prospect of living in the same building as my dear friend.

Bill made the home-buying process seem easy and took care of all the fine details. He showed us a two-bedroom, two-bathroom condo on the ninth floor at 1555 Lakeside Drive. It had floor-to-ceiling glass doors and windows that overlooked the entirety of Lake Merritt and received abundant light. I loved it. We moved in in March 1994. Patrick was as delighted as I was, especially because his first cousin Andrew and his wife, Patricia, lived just down the hall from us. Kamala was on the mezzanine level with an equally awesome view of the lake.

It was a spectacular time in our lives. We were both active and busy and flush with all the excitement of that early adult independence. As a priceless bonus, I never felt alone, for though Kamala and I were carving out very different life paths for ourselves, on any given evening I would just pop down to her condo carrying a glass of wine to chat with her and catch up while she cooked. I remember she had a large, stunning framed painting in the foyer of her condo. It was of one of the Hindu gods—I believe it was Shiva. She noticed me gazing at it one time and explained a little bit about it. I'm drawn toward all things with a spiritual bent and had always loved hearing snippets about her Indian traditions and faith.

Lauren and our toddler son, Patrick Jr.—then three years old—also loved to take the elevator down to Auntie Kamala's to hang out with her for a little while. On the weekends we'd step out to the path around the lake and teach the children how to ride their bikes together. She's always been great with kids, and both of mine just adored hanging out at her place. Thinking back on their combined laughter always makes me feel good. That time is held fast in my mind as one of the happiest and most memorable spans of my life.

I loved the convenience of simply meeting her in the lobby, jumping in her car or mine, and going shopping. Our tastes were perfectly, sometimes eerily, aligned on all kinds of things. We coincidentally each bought a black BMW 325i. Given our family situations, hers was a convertible while mine was a four-door sedan—but it was nonetheless a surprise, as neither of us knew the other had bought a new car until we were both driving them around the parking garage of our building. As is our knowing, near-telepathic way of communicating, we just looked at each other in disbelief and started laughing.

One Christmas, Kamala called and said she wanted to come over to show me something she had just bought—which was curious, as I told her I also wanted to show her something I had just treated myself to. I'd splurged and bought myself a black, three-quarter-length dress coat that was well beyond my budget but that just felt like one of those items I *had* to have. I put my coat on to show it off to her when she arrived. She came in and, before she could register what I was wearing, excitedly said, "Look at my new coat!" It was almost identical to mine; hers was just the full-length version! She stepped back and looked me up and down, our eyes met and got big, and we both cracked up, filling the room with laughter.

We always enjoyed a good shopping session. When the department store I. Magnin announced it was closing for good, Kamala and I carved out a day to go visit the downtown Oakland location one last time. This was the mid-1990s, and we were establishing ourselves in our careers. It was that stage in life when one finds the theme song to *The Jeffersons*, "Movin' On Up," particularly resonant. Having both inherited the drive and ambition of our mothers, we were young women working hard for everything we had.

I can still hear the sound of us laughing as we rode to the store together in Kamala's BMW (we lived close enough to walk, but had made the joint decision that we were definitely going to need a car for all the stuff we'd be coming home with). As we approached the prominent emerald-green art deco landmark we saw a line of (primarily) women wrapped around the corner of Broadway and Twentieth Street. We knew we were in for quite the shopping spree, with everything having been marked down to 80 percent off. We chatted away while we waited in the long line, then, as soon as we finally got in there, Kamala and I quickly and systematically flipped through hanging garments and those that had been tossed on the ground. She'd veer away in one direction while

I drifted off in another, then occasionally we'd reconnect along the crowded aisles with arms full: "What do you think of this, Stacey? I think Maya will like it," she'd say, showing me a petite skirt suit she had picked out for her sister. I'd nod in agreement, meanwhile caught up in the frenzy and going overboard—carrying around a couple of pairs of slacks for work, several blouses and dresses, even a satin halter wedding dress (the price had been reduced to such a ridiculously low amount that Kamala and I agreed it didn't make sense *not* to get it…after all, you never know when you might need an extra wedding dress)!

After what seemed like a full day of canvassing the entire store, we huddled in a corner and conducted our process of elimination. The checkout line was just as long as the line to enter the store. I still remember the two of us holding our breath as the clerk tallied up my stack. But we walked out laughing, feeling quite accomplished. The high cost I'd shelled out would be a motivation, I rationalized. I'd cover the bill by working that much harder to have an especially good sales month.

It was within my grasp to do so, given the nature of the work that I had entered at the time—thanks largely to the influence and insistence of my mom. I had ended up following a similar technical path, and I was doing so with all the ambition that I had inherited from her. I quickly went from being an operator to becoming a customer instructor, my first management-level position at Pacific Bell in downtown Oakland.

Shortly before my interview for that job was the moment when I finally decided that stuttering was not going to determine any part of my life. I wasn't in middle school, as my mom had been, nor did my determination nearly start a race riot. Rather, it was when I was applying to be a customer instructor. Part of the interview process involved demonstrating to my prospective boss and his team how I would train them to set up their phones and use voice mail (this was in the early nineties). I remember praying hard as I waited my turn to go into the intimidating boardroom, asking the Holy Spirit to please help me not to stutter. A calmness settled over me that I had never felt before. I entered the room with confidence and was hired for the position.

To this day I still feel it when a stutter is coming on or when it's about to trip me up. But I have trained myself to simply pause and take a breath when I need to—no matter how long that takes—before finishing what I have to say. As long as I take a moment and do not let myself feel panicked by the silence, my brain can catch up and determine what I mean to say.

I was delighted with my new job. I had the freedom to make my own schedule and loved going on-site to train customers on their new Centrex and voice mail systems. It's not for everyone, but it suited my interests and skill set.

My cubicle was across from the team of system design consultants (SDCs), who designed data networks for business customers. I overheard their conversations with company engineers and became intrigued by their work. Like my mom, I was fascinated by how voice and data could travel far distances over copper lines and fiber optics.

Doris had retired as an engineer, so I asked her to teach me about the technology. She gave me a good overview; I just needed to connect the dots between what she had explained to me and the various new product names. I asked one of the SDCs if he would help. The combination of my mom's foundation and his explanation, delivered over a whiteboard training session, helped me make sense of it, and I started staying up at night to study the products.

A few months later, the company presented an opportunity: those who could pass a written assessment would be eligible to interview for a technical sales consultant (TSC) position. After all my prep work, I felt ready to give it a try. I scored among the highest in California and landed the position. I absolutely loved the new work. This was right at the start of the dot-com era, and the time couldn't have been better to be in a data sales role. I went on to design some of the largest internet service provider (ISP) networks, progressed to designing hospital networks, and was promoted to managing Pacific Bell's health-care organization for Northern California—one of my most rewarding career phases.

*　　*　　*

Kamala, meanwhile, had gone from being a prosecutor in Alameda to working in the district attorney's office in San Francisco. She quickly established herself and was on her way. Much like our mothers, we connected over being extremely devoted to the work that we were doing. But whenever we actually got the chance to sit down and be together, we rarely used that time to discuss our jobs. She might briefly mention major cases or work politics, or I might tell her what was happening with me on my travels in the field, and she would laugh about the technicality of my job. But by and large, it's not as if we sat and discussed her decision to become a prosecutor or her stance on capital punishment—any more than we would discuss data circuits or ISP networks. That wasn't the nature of our friendship. Our deep familiarity enabled us to just totally be ourselves. Our catching up was used as a relief from our respective daily grinds. We'd go out to dinner in the city, settle into the familiarity of being together, and talk about dating, or she would ask about my kids, or we'd talk about our friends and parents—occasionally sprinkling in reminiscences about our formative younger days.

———

One of the strongest threads we share, and which I share with many of my close girlfriends, is the love and support we feel for our mothers, our aunties, and the maternal figures who helped raise us. In 1996, our last full year of living in the condo together (Patrick and I moved out in 1997), Kamala asked me to help her host a Mother's Day brunch downstairs at her place. I thought it was a lovely idea and was excited to help.

Our condominium building always had a festive ambience, and our moms loved coming over. I hosted some of my kids' birthday parties in its clubhouse and often held get-togethers in our unit on the ninth floor. The entrance to 1555 Lakeside Drive had an impressive curved driveway, and the landscaping was kept immaculate. There was something innately convivial about the atmosphere there, you felt it from the moment you walked in. Many of the doormen had worked there for decades, and they would greet those of us who lived there by name and with a bit of a chat. All of them always treated guests (especially our moms) with the same level of respect and class.

A few nights after she asked, when we were both done with work, I popped down to Kamala's unit to plan the brunch. We sat at her kitchen table sharing menu ideas as we reminisced about our moms, then discussed what they would appreciate the most for Mother's Day. We decided to keep it simple and relaxed (fruit and cheese plates, vegetable trays, a couple of her fabulous dips, and deviled eggs), then we divvied up our shopping lists. I asked my mom for her fabulous chili bean dip recipe, and Kamala said she'd make a baked polenta dish. Needless to say, we'd have bubbles and OJ for mimosas; what's a brunch without mimosas?!

Early that Sunday, I went downstairs to help Kamala set up. There wasn't much for me to do, since she always kept her unit looking elegant. The living room curtains were open wide, displaying the view of Lake Merritt, and a soft May breeze flowed in from the cracked bay windows as jazz played softly in the background. We really wanted our mothers and godmothers to feel special and appreciated. Kamala adored her mommy, I felt the same about mine, and we were both excited for the opportunity to celebrate them and all those from our Berkeley village who had contributed to the women we had become.

Kamala carefully arranged fresh-cut flowers on her dining table. Taller stems of fresh flowers sat in a large vase on her glass coffee table in the living room. Coincidentally, we were both wearing gold pants, which we laughed about as we chatted and waited for our moms.

That day felt so special that the memories have remained especially vivid in my mind, down to what everybody was wearing. My mom was one of the first guests to arrive, looking sharp as ever in an off-white skirt suit, nylons, and pumps. Shyamala arrived soon after, wearing lightweight, wide-legged burgundy pants and a taupe sweater top. Aunt Mary always dressed comfortably, but with her own sense of flair. She was in plum-colored cotton pants, a purple top, and a multi-colored jacket. It was incredible to witness how quickly my mom and Shyamala reconnected, even though it had been a while since they had spent real time together. In no time they were sitting down together, talking and laughing as boisterously as they always had.

Freddy came along with Aunt Mary, and some other close friends of Shyamala's showed up as well. Maya, Meena, and my two kids were there. Everything went off without a hitch as this force of mothers and children gathered together, enjoying the hors d'oeuvres, a couple of mimosas, and the long-familiar company of one another. Kamala's creamy baked polenta was delicious—I have a bright memory of her pulling it out of the oven, sizzling, and covering it with a thick layer of sauteed mushrooms as she carried on chatting and catching up with everybody.

Afterward she came over and sat on the carpet with my son Patrick, who had just turned five years old. Maya had also gotten comfortable, shoes off, and was sitting in a floral dress, flipping through photo albums and laughing. Meena and Lauren were watching television in the bedroom and I was floating around, snapping pictures and chiming in on side conversations. It felt as it always does with the best of family occasions. It's those simple, intimate occasions that eventually mean so much. Reflecting on it welcomes that same light breeze into my memories—and much as I can visualize everybody's outfit, I can hear the warm buzz of chatter and laughter, so clearly it could be in the next room.

It was a wonderful day, respecting and honoring the most crucial women who had helped raise us, along with those we were now raising! From my perspective, it was the pinnacle event of our time living by the lake. Although Kamala and I only stayed there together for just under four years, so much memorable, quality time was shared on Lakeside Drive. The coming years would bring a series of crushing emotional blows, making our years by the Lake seem especially joyous by contrast. It was a precious time, as we were both forging our own paths, working hard to get there, and we were supported no matter what—confident in and blessed by the knowledge that a true friend's company was a mere elevator ride away.

Compassion

Growing through Grief

Naturally, over the course of a full life and a full friendship, challenging spans will present themselves—times when support, counsel, and just quiet understanding are appreciated more than anything. It's those inevitable dark moments of life when true friendship is revealed, far more than in the moments when you're having fun or one is helping the other with her wardrobe.

One of the most painful periods of my life was set in motion the weekend before my mother and father-in-law's shared birthday, August 7, in 2006. My mother had planned a large party to be held in my parents' backyard. Her excitement was palpable: she had been talking about having a large outdoor birthday party for years, and she even ordered new furniture for the occasion when we were finally making it happen. Her birthday fell on a Monday that year, so we decided that we would hold the party the following weekend.

By this point Patrick and I had separated, but we had done so on very amicable terms, and we always came together for family events. He had decided that he was going to drive up to Guerneville, in Northern California, for the weekend to attend the Reggae on the River festival with a friend. It struck me as odd that he had rented an RV to drive all the way up to Guerneville for a reggae festival—he had always been almost exclusively a jazz fan, and besides, this was the weekend before the big birthday party. The weekend passed, Sunday came and went, and neither our kids nor I heard from him. Monday, August 7 arrived—both his father's and my mother's birthday—and still, not a word from Patrick.

By Tuesday, without anyone having had contact with him, every member of his very large family, and mine, was deeply concerned. His friends, brothers, sisters, and I called his cell phone hundreds of times. I was parked outside the Rite Aid in Orinda, and I thought I'd give it another try. Finally somebody picked up the phone, but then there was just silence on the other end. All I could make out was slight grunts and the sound of him clearing his throat. I knew it was he, but I had never heard such a terrifying sound.

"Patrick, is that you? Are you there? Are you OK? What's going on, who are you with, where are you?" I asked frantically.

Deafening silence was the only response before the line was dropped. I went to dial it again, but just then I received a call from one of his sisters, Lisa, who relayed that their other sister, Ingrid (who we call Jane), had also managed to get through and had received the same response of grunts and silence. Equally overwhelmed by the same helplessness I had just felt, Jane had thought quickly and said, "Patrick, if this is you and you need help, press a button on the phone." She heard the tone of a button being pressed, then he hung up the line. Something was terribly, terribly wrong.

She'd tracked down the number of Patrick's friend with whom he had driven up to Guerneville, and she had demanded that he drive Patrick home immediately, no matter what state he was in. I picked up our fifteen-year-old son from St. Mary's, and the two of us drove straight to Patrick's mom's house in El Cerrito. By the time we arrived, a police car was blocking the street. I pulled into the first parking spot I saw and had a quick word with the officer, and the two of us ran inside. Patrick had just been at the house, but his sister had immediately called 911, and the ambulance had taken him to Doctors Medical Center in San Pablo. Nobody was sure what was wrong with him, and he had been unable to speak.

We sped to the hospital and waited there for hours, anxiously awaiting the diagnosis. After what felt like ages, it was determined that Patrick had experienced some kind of a hemorrhage, and as a result his brain was covered with blood. Lauren, who was home from her first year at Hampton University (in Virginia) for summer break, met us at the hospital. Lauren, Patrick, and I gathered around Patrick Sr. in the emergency room. He was obviously trying hard to say something, but no words were coming out of his mouth. All he could do was move his hand as if he were turning the steering wheel of a car.

After consultations with doctors and several attempts at trying to communicate, it became clear that he was not going to recover anytime soon. He was only forty-two years old. Things had been going well for him, and he had been excited about having recently started his own tile company, Deanco Tile (named for his middle name, Dean), which was just starting to take off and develop a reputation. Our son, Patrick, was only a freshman in high school; he adored his dad and loved being the "junior" version of him, by name and by likeness.

With so much uncertainty surrounding if and when he would ever recover, Lauren felt profoundly conflicted about whether she should go back to Hampton or just attend college locally. She had been accepted to UC Berkeley, and once again my father ("Papa" to her) was insistent that she should have gone there, perhaps hoping she would listen to him where I had ignored his and Uncle Sherman's advice. He urged her to reapply. She felt very torn and asked me if I thought she should stay home. "No," I told her without pause. She had had a wonderful first year at Hampton, and we were going to continue as planned.

Her father and I had helped her move into the dorm a year prior, though it felt as if much longer than a year had passed. Even though we were separated, we always got along, and we were invariably in sync when it came to our kids. Though our marriage was not meant to be, we were always partners in parenting and had gotten back to being the good friends we had started off as. I knew Patrick inside out, and I had no doubt that he would want her to return to the college she loved. I told her as much.

Patrick was kept at UCSF Medical Center for several months. Tragically, he was ultimately transferred to a nursing and rehabilitation center in Alameda, where he has remained since 2006. There's never been a great deal of clarity on what precisely caused the brain aneurysm. We had recently lost his cousin Joey, "Big Joe," with whom Patrick had been incredibly close. I had known Joey even before I met Patrick—it was he who had gotten the two of us together. Everyone loved him, and his sudden death had weighed heavily on us all, but it had been especially crushing for Patrick. I wondered if the anguish over Joey's death had anything to do with it.

What happened to Patrick is the most devastating experience I've had to endure. It has had an overwhelming, ongoing effect on me, my children, and our close friends. Kamala and Patrick had always gotten along very well and enjoyed spending time together when we lived in the condo by the lake. She was shocked by the news, like everybody. Early on, she and my other friends would ask about him, and they were very supportive and ready to offer any help I needed, but for a long while, we just didn't know whether he might come out of it. There was only so much anybody could do.

By the time his brain caught up, his body had atrophied, leaving him unable to move at all. But he regained his memory, and today he can carry on conversations from his nursing home. I told him about Kamala's campaign and he was delighted, just saying, "*Kamala Harris!*" He and I go all the way back to high school, and he has known her for practically as long as he's known me, and he is cognizant that she's our vice president. But it's just so tragic. Patrick was one of the most dynamic people: active, vibrant, and so loved by so many people. For him to remain in this state—it's still an impossible situation for me to fathom.

Patrick's aneurysm was only the beginning of a stretch of my life that was marked by a string of losses, which consumed all of my time and energy—while also making me far more inclined to hold tight to my loved ones, recognize who my genuine friends are, and cherish the time spent with them.

———

In 2008, just as I was coming up for air from the realization of Patrick's condition and fate and what they would mean for our family, Uncle Sherman passed away. He went suddenly, from a heart attack. Aunt Mary noticed that he had been in the bathroom for too long, and by the time she went to check on him, he was already gone.

My parents drove to their apartment as soon as they heard, but my father was too upset over the loss of a man he viewed as his brother and was unable to even get out of the car. So my mom went in to talk with Mary and to begin helping her arrange matters. Uncle Sherman, who had been so central to my young life, was the first from their close-knit Berkeley group to go. It came as a shock to the whole community, of which he was such a central figure.

We all gathered together at Geoffrey's Inner Circle—a banquet hall in downtown Oakland—for his memorial service. My parents, Shyamala, Kamala, Maya, Ronny, and I sat together around a small round table in the back of the ballroom, talking about Uncle Sherman and the legend he had been for all of us, especially throughout the childhood of those of us from the younger generation. As the last line of his obituary stated, "Concerned, loving, caring, he was an incomparable mentor to the many children and young people who knew him as 'Uncle Sherman.'"

It was healing for all of us to be gathered there, honoring his extraordinary presence. Maya suggested to Doris that we all get together again at my parents' house in Berkeley, as we used to. My mom and Shyamala were excited about the idea of a reunion, given the comfort of being together again, despite the somber occasion.

Months passed, with my mom periodically mentioning to me that we needed to follow through and invite everyone over to the house. She kept saying that Shyamala was on her mind. Late that spring, I mentioned to her that my cousin Alberta and I were going to take a walk around Lake Merritt, and she asked me to please stop by and check on Shyamala, who lived near the lake at that stage of her life. Mom recalls how much Shyamala loved that condo on Bellevue Avenue, just across the street from the lake. She loved her view and being centrally located to everything. I was more than happy to stop by and approached the door with a big smile on my face.

Meena, Maya's daughter, answered alongside Shyamala. It was immediately obvious that Shyamala was not well. Her hair had thinned significantly, and her face—usually filled with light and curiosity—seemed drawn. By her appearance, I suspected that she was undergoing chemo. But I didn't know what to say or do, so I just tried to behave normally and have a bit of a chat. It was far briefer than it would have been had she been her usual self. After we left, my cousin, who worked at Alameda Hospital and saw patients every day, echoed my suspicion. I called my mom as soon as we got home and told her I'd seen Shyamala and that she should call her right away.

It had been more than a decade since Kamala and I had sold our condos at 1555 Lakeside Drive (a regret we've since laughed about, noting what happened to real estate value in the Bay Area). She was living in another condo she had bought, south of Market Street in San Francisco, and was serving as the city's district attorney.

I had bought a house in El Sobrante, in Contra Costa County, and was working hard, managing my job as well as possible in order to pay for my son's and daughter's tuitions. With their father in a nursing home, it was up to me to take care of their education. More than anything, Patrick and I wanted our children to attend the schools of their choice and to graduate from college. Anything less was not an option in my mind. With Lauren set to graduate that spring and Patrick Jr. graduating high school and planning to attend Cal State Northridge for college, I was halfway to the finish line my husband and I had established. Getting there was a relentless, constant grind, even requiring at one point that I move back in with my parents to regroup and save money. But I was determined to get both of my children through.

That kept me extremely busy, in terms of both my schedule and my preoccupations. Meanwhile, Kamala's career was accelerating. With equally hectic lives at that stage, Kamala and I didn't talk as often—though we continued to meet for dinner in San Francisco after work every few months to catch up. One night, I remember going out to dinner at Maya, a Mexican restaurant on Second Street, in South of Market in San Francisco. We were chatting away until somebody caught Kamala's eye, and her voice dropped. "Don't look now," she said, "but the man behind you is the defending attorney for the Diane Whipple case."

The case was over a recent, highly publicized tragedy in which a young woman carrying her groceries into her Pacific Heights apartment had been mauled to death by two dogs. The dog owners were two attorneys themselves, and the Bay Area had been shocked by what had happened and what the consequences would be. Kamala and I quietly discussed how devastating it was. Whipple had been around our age, making it feel more personal. But it was a deeply complicated case. I was very conflicted because I knew that the dogs would be put down, which has always been a hard pill for me to swallow. The conversation stands out in my mind because we so rarely discussed the law or her work. Kamala wasn't yet as involved as she later would be. (In the end, she would oversee the case for years.)

That discussion was an outlier. We would usually just catch each other up on what was happening in our personal lives, and it never failed to restore me. No matter what the subject was, no matter how emotional we might become, our conversations would always be threaded with the boisterous yet tender laughter we've always shared. There's an understanding between us, an intuitive awareness of each other.

After I saw Shyamala that day, I realized how much time had passed since Kamala and I had had the opportunity to be together. I knew it was important to reconnect whenever we could, so we scheduled one of our catch-up dinners.

Shyamala passed away shortly after, on February 11, 2009. The memorial service, held in a lovely hall within Shyamala's condominium—a historic building overlooking Lake Merritt—was beautiful, and it was a fitting tribute to this extraordinary woman. I went with my mother and father. Though my mother had always talked about Shyamala's accomplishments ever since I was a child, I was startled and filled with awe to hear it all again as she was eulogized by her closest friends and colleagues. It was amazing to listen to them pay tribute to her singular life and to just sit there—especially then, as a working mother—and consider her achievements.

I tried to imagine what it would have been like for her to receive her undergraduate degree at nineteen years old, and to tell her grandparents—as the eldest girl in the family—that she wanted to get her PhD from Berkeley, in nutrition and endocrinology. She achieved that by age twenty-five, the same year she gave birth to Kamala. Then she gave her whole life to finding a cure for cancer and to raising her beloved girls. Shyamala had always been a marvel to me, just based on her presence, but I hadn't spent much time viscerally understanding how much strength it had required for her to become a world-renowned scientist while simultaneously raising two exceptional daughters.

As I absorbed the colorful stories from people who had known her at each stage of her impressive life, my personal memories came flooding back—like memories of the times I would pick Kamala up to go out dancing. I got my driver's license much sooner than she did, so I wouldn't hesitate to make the thirty-minute drive from Berkeley to their house in East Oakland to pick her up, and then we'd either head back to Berkeley or go into San Francisco. Shyamala would ask for details about where we were going and whom we'd be meeting, remind us to be very careful, and always give me *that look*. Shyamala did not play, and she could always see right through any nonsense.

At her memorial, looking around and noticing her brother and sisters from India, smelling the incredible spread of traditional Indian food that was waiting for all of us, I was transported briefly to their visits when we were growing up. My parents and I would drive out to Shyamala's, where Aunt Mary and Uncle Sherman would meet us. Shyamala, a phenomenal cook, would always have a wide assortment of Indian dishes prepared. Her home smelled incredible—warm, distinct, and inviting. It felt like a special treat anytime we went over there for the holidays to celebrate. My mom and I *loved* her bourbon balls...I would always sneak a few extra of those! The two of us still talk about those tremendous recipes of hers, dishes only Shyamala could create. Her presence was so distinct, so magical, that it just felt impossible to wrap my head around the notion that she was gone, even as I was sitting at her funeral.

Kamala rose to speak and delivered a eulogy I will never forget, offering a series of anecdotes that revealed Shyamala's courage, wisdom, humor, and loving spirit. Of course I had heard Kamala's public addresses, especially recently, throughout her campaign to become district attorney. I'd been there for enough events to know that she is an excellent, poised speaker. But I also knew how much she adored her mother—she'll be the first one to reiterate that she meant the world to her—and I knew how profoundly painful this loss was for her. Shyamala had been her top supporter throughout her entire life, from her childhood to her career. Before she even began to speak, my eyes filled with tears, though I tried to fight them back. Kamala, as ever, remained strong and self-possessed as she imparted touching stories about being raised by such an inspirational woman. Knowing how deep both her love and her hurt were in that moment, I felt the deepest respect for my dear friend.

A dozen years later, after she was chosen as Biden's running mate, I was often asked (in brief media interviews) what

I admired most about Kamala. The list is a long one, and I could never even scratch the surface or begin to peel back all of the history between us, certainly not within the ninety seconds I was given to respond. But among those qualities would be her courage, compassion, and generous spirit—even in the face of great hardship. All of these qualities were on display as she held it together and memorialized the brilliant light that was her mother. The generosity of her love especially shone through in how she finished her tribute. I still get chills thinking about it.

At the end of her eulogy, Kamala told the packed room how much Shyamala loved all kinds of music, but that her mommy's favorite song was "Oh Happy Day," the 1968 song by the Edwin Hawkins Singers.

As she remained standing, the infectious tune came over the speakers, and Kamala started clapping to the beat. Without hesitation or meditation, we all rose to our feet and started clapping along with her, most people crying, smiling, and singing our way through it together. Looking around the room, seeing her family and friends, smelling the warm food I associated with her home, while all of us clapped and danced to an exuberant contemporary gospel hymn…the whole scene represented how beautifully Shyamala had blended their worlds and embraced the best of them all, amid the melting pot of Berkeley where she had made a life for herself and her daughters. It was a perfect, unforgettable, moving way to praise and bid farewell to Shyamala's indomitable spirit.

> Oh happy day
> Oh happy day
> When Jesus washed
> Oh, when he washed
> When Jesus washed
> He washed my sins away
> Oh happy day....
> He taught me how to watch, fight, and pray
> Fight and pray!
> And live rejoicing every day

———

Just before 11:00 p.m. on September 4, 2012, my cell phone rang. "Who would be calling me this late? No one calls me this late," I thought. I got up, went over to my phone, saw that it was Kamala, and picked it up immediately.

She paused for a moment, then I heard her take a deep breath before delivering her news. "Aunt Mary passed away," she said. I instantly heard the devastation in her voice. There was little to explain or discuss. Unable to fully grasp the news myself, I assured her I was there to help with whatever needed to be done. She thanked me and suggested we start with their home. I told her I'd be there in the morning.

Aunt Mary and Uncle Sherman's small, two-bedroom apartment was cluttered. There was a whole lot of history in there to unpack. Kamala and I just looked at each other; there was little to be said and plenty to do. Much like our mothers, we share the capacity to focus on a task and get a job done. Without much consulting on how we were going to go about it, we surveyed the whole apartment together, beginning to organize as we walked silently through the middle room that was part office, part sewing room, part den. As the two of us slowly made our way through each room, I was taken aback by the stacks of papers and miscellaneous items everywhere. Where would we even begin to sort through this? There was a small bedroom in front where Sherman's clothes and coats still were, along with their many, many books. Rolling up our sleeves, we spent the first day organizing their things into stacks on the floor to pack in boxes, then spent a few hours sorting through the clothes. After about an hour or so Kamala said she'd get started on their bedroom, and I moved to the front room, searching for important papers worth keeping, such as their wills and any medical forms.

At one point I went to the bedroom to check on Kamala. She was sitting on the edge of their unmade bed, flipping through papers and envelopes. The ambience was so eerily absent of the warmth and life that had once filled it. It was all the more jarring to realize that both Aunt Mary and Uncle Sherman had exhaled for the last time in that home. Something about being in their bedroom made that especially potent. "Oh my," I said softly.

"I know," Kamala replied simply, with sadness in her voice. We looked at each other for a few seconds in silence, sighed together, and got back to work.

In addition to clearing out Sherman and Mary's apartment, we set about making the necessary arrangements to honor her life. Throughout that time, as I gathered information about Aunt Mary's accomplishments, I had a growing sense of regret that I hadn't spent more time with her and Uncle Sherman so I could have asked more questions about their full and fascinating lives. At the same time, it filled me with gratitude to glean little details about this incredible woman Kamala and I had grown up around. Many of the details I learned were shared with me by Aubrey LaBrie.

Among her many ambitions was the desire to travel to Cuba. Aunt Mary was a woman who made her ambitions her reality. She made the trip and visited medical and social welfare facilities, performing arts institutes, and all levels of schools and colleges. Later, she returned to the country with a group of citizens from Oakland led by Congresswoman Barbara Lee. During that trip Mary experienced one of the greatest thrills of her life, the opportunity to meet President Fidel Castro. Her picture of him is one of the souvenirs I kept aside as Kamala and I boxed up the apartment. I also set aside Uncle Sherman's chess set for Kamala, remembering the twinkling smile in his eyes as he taught her how to play chess. I knew she'd appreciate it, and she confirmed as much by sending a text thanking me for thinking of it.

On the second day, we met at the apartment again and devoted the bulk of our time to their colossal quantity of books. Given Aunt Mary's passion and background in education, we donated their extraordinary collection to Contra Costa College, where she had worked for a while and through which she managed to make it to Japan.

We decided to hold Aunt Mary's service at Geoffrey's Inner Circle, the same place Uncle Sherman's memorial had been held and the last place we had all been together. But first we had to let go of her body.

Kamala called and asked me to be there with her for Aunt Mary's cremation on Tuesday, September 18. My father, who still thought of her as family from the Berkeley days and wanted to be there for Kamala and me, asked to come along. I called and left a message and sent a text to let Kamala know. She responded, **Hey honey, got your message…love, love.** So I picked Dad up from my parents' house to ride with him to Fremont. We were running a few minutes late, so I focused intently on the road. My dad and I were unusually quiet during the drive, reflecting on the gravity of what we were about to do.

I swung into the parking lot and immediately spotted

and pulled up next to the black SUV that Kamala had been driven in by her security team. I knew which way to walk—around a small beige building toward a patio—and there she was, sitting on a bench, holding a rumpled tissue. "Hey, Kamala," I said in a low, gentle voice. Dad eased up behind me and greeted her as well. "Hi, Robert," she replied, looking up. Eye contact between the two of us sufficed. Then, without a word, she looked beyond us. My eyes followed her sad gaze and paused on the wooden coffin sitting about six feet away from us. A surreal feeling came over me.

Against my own will, I started imagining what Aunt Mary might look like in that box, down to details I couldn't stop myself from wondering about: Were her eyes open or closed? Had somebody folded her hands, or were they straight along the sides of her body? Was she wrapped in a cloth? I knew nothing about the cremation process aside from having seen urns after the fact.

Kamala's longtime security agents stood at a respectful distance. Making eye contact, I smiled softly at them. Dad and I sat quietly next to Kamala, and the three of us gazed at the coffin and the grounds beyond. Aside from the occasional chirping of birds, it was quiet and still. I put my right hand on Kamala's shoulder, trying to communicate my support through my touch. I knew what it meant for her to say goodbye to this remarkable woman who had imparted to Kamala so much love, time, and wisdom.

Looking around, I wondered what might happen next. Shortly a man approached from within the small building and asked if we were ready. Kamala nodded, affirming to him that it was time. Two men lifted the wooden coffin, placed it in what looked like a large outdoor stone oven, and closed the opening. I followed Kamala slowly as she stood up and walked over.

When we were making the initial arrangements for Aunt Mary, Kamala had told me about the Hindu belief that the soul is freed once the body has been cremated. Shyamala had once said something similar to my mom, about how she just couldn't understand the custom of keeping a body preserved for a funeral. Her belief was also that one should be cremated as quickly as possible, to release the soul from the body. That thought ran through my mind, bringing with it the hope of solace—both for Kamala and for Aunt Mary's spirit.

Kamala raised her right hand to press the "Start" button, then hesitated for a brief second. I grasped her left hand, and Daddy stood about five feet behind us, to my left. After pausing, she took a breath, then pressed it. We stood there a few minutes, then walked back to the patio area. I marveled at her will, her courage, and her composure. With little to say, we embraced and headed to our cars. Driving there, I hadn't been sure how I would feel, and I had been nervous about the whole process. But as we drove home, I felt awash in an unexpected sense of peace and closure. Somewhere within me I truly felt as if Aunt Mary, and her big, beautiful soul, had been set free.

My father was the next to pass on. He died at home, in my parents' bedroom, on April 17, 2014, ten days before my fiftieth birthday. Mom had just made their morning coffee and brought my dad's cup to him. She went back to the kitchen, and by the time she returned to the bedroom he was slumped over on his left side. It was fitting for him to pass away peacefully, like Uncle Sherman, at home with the woman he had loved for almost his entire life, finally at rest in his beloved Berkeley.

I was working at the time and was on a conference call as my mom was trying to reach me. I had been observing Daddy's declining physical abilities taking their toll on him over the past few years, partially because of his bad knee. The cartilage in both knees was worn down to nothing, but his right knee was especially bad, bone rubbing against bone. I have the same issue, unfortunately, with the cartilage worn down in both my knees due to decades of running and skiing. He had refused to try surgery years prior, a stubbornness my mom thinks may have been due to his own mother declining after she underwent what was supposed to be a minor surgery on her knee. She had fallen getting off the bus, was operated on, and soon after suffered a stroke and was never the same. She passed away at the age of sixty-three from a heart attack. But my dad always traced her death back to the surgery and subsequent stroke.

Daddy's knee issue had made it incredibly painful for him to walk at all. He had slowed down to barely being able to go grocery shopping, which had always been one of his favorite things to do. He had become confined to a chair in my parents' bedroom, watching TV and reading the daily newspapers. I had found it deeply painful to watch, as he had always been such an extrovert and social being. His spirit seemed broken by his paralyzed body, and I hadn't been able to imagine him lasting much longer in such a way. But no matter how mentally prepared I'd thought I was, hearing the news that my dad had passed away was devastating beyond description.

I barely got any sleep for the week that followed. Ronny and I helped Mom with all the arrangements, but managing the dozens and dozens of phone calls became emotionally draining. We received help from close friends, but there was only so much they could do.

Kamala called me every day that week, which ended with the memorial for my dad. As busy as I knew she was, she still found time to talk with me at length, every day. She had of course endured the same kind of anguish when Shyamala had passed, followed by Aunt Mary. She knew me, knew my dad, cared for him deeply, and understood what I was going through. She had tried her best to rearrange her schedule so she could attend his service, but she was booked to speak at a university and couldn't get out of it. I had insisted that I understood, and I really did. The fact that she made a point of checking in with me daily was more than enough support for me.

The night before my dad's funeral I was at Kinko's, making copies of the obituaries and the memorial programs. It was around nine o'clock and there were maybe two or three people there. I was standing at the counter, confirming the quantity and getting ready to pay. Kamala's call arrived just then, catching me at one of my weariest moments. I stepped away from the counter and went to the corner to talk.

"How you doing, honey?"

"I'm losing it," I told her, trying to hold back tears. "I'm just having such a hard time keeping it together." I let go and started crying. I felt so unstable—not as if I were about to crack, just exhausted. I could hardly see straight. It had been such a hectic week, with me constantly running around. That's to be expected, of course. I'd had to deal with the mortuary, the funeral arrangements, the caterer, and writing the obituary—which had been emotionally draining. Then there were all the phone calls, coming in constantly, and constant texts that I had yet to respond to.

What was unexpected was my mom's state. She was

completely distraught. I had never seen her like that. She couldn't make a decision about anything. This is a woman who had always been so decisive and in charge of everything...so it was a real shock for my brother and me to see her like that. I don't fault or blame her at all; this was the love of her life. But it did make me feel as if I had to be especially strong, for my mom and for my kids. When Kamala called that night, I was finally able to collapse, in a way. She let me cry, which felt as comforting as an embrace.

"I just haven't had hardly any sleep," I continued. "And I tried to prepare myself, but the reality is still so hard. I'm trying to get everything right, but there's just been so much to do." As always, she asked how she could help.

"Is there anything I can do? Anything at all?"

"No, no. I think I've got it all under control. I just have to finish with the printing. Lauren and Shawn"—her husband— "just arrived and they're out in the car. They'll help with whatever's left."

I knew she was with me in spirit, which in itself gave me a sense of strength. I could get through this.

———

We held the service at the chapel of the Sunset View Cemetery & Mortuary in El Cerrito, with a standing-room-only crowd. Cards and flowers had come from people we hadn't seen or heard from in years (and from several I didn't know at all).

My brother and I both spoke, recalling many examples of lessons learned from Dad. I shared stories from the glorious childhood that he had provided for us. I realize that few others are able to speak as positively about their upbringing, and how unusually lucky I was, so I generally refrain from talking about it at length. But I wanted everybody to know what an extraordinary father and papa he had been, always placing family first.

My daughter, Lauren, also offered a heartfelt eulogy, talking about how it seemed like yesterday that Grandma would pick her and Patrick up from St. Joseph's—in that same '66 Mustang—and take them to Stannage (which is how we often refer to my parents' house, as it's the name of their street). There they'd look forward to Papa's delicious red beans and rice. She recalled how much Papa made her laugh, and how he read the newspaper every day, making sure she and Patrick Jr. knew about everything going on, often cutting out relevant clippings to send to them. They had both learned so much from all he had accomplished, the places he had traveled, the stories he had told.

Lauren shared one of the last things he sent her, her horoscope from a recent month, one offering a message that rang especially true to my ears. It stated, "Rely on where you come from and how you were raised to guide you in the right direction." She finished by offering one of her favorite quotes: "The love of a family is life's greatest blessing."

———

Patrick Jr. was expected to graduate from college a few months later, at the end of the academic year in 2014, so I decided to relocate to the LA area to help support him as he began pursuing an acting career. I had lived in the Bay Area my whole life and was ready for a change myself.

Shortly after I had moved into a home in Arcadia with my son, I heard my father's voice. It was just before dawn, in that calm space between being asleep and being awake. I heard three or four hard knocks, then my dad's voice: "Stacey, it's me, Daddy." I thought I must have been veering into a dream, but was fully conscious when I heard his voice again: "Stacey, open the door, it's Daddy." There was no mistaking it. It was *his* voice. I lay in bed, feeling paralyzed; I wanted to respond, but I was too emotionally startled to move.

I can't be sure how much time passed before I was able to get up and walk to Patrick's room.

"Did you hear...a knock on the door?" I asked him.

"Yes," he said immediately. "Yes, and I heard Papa."

I took a deep breath in the darkness, then walked back to my room slowly. I miss my father from the depths of my heart and forever will. Though hearing his voice had given me a jolt, my feeling about it evolved into a sense of profound relief. It served as a blessing and a balm. Since that evening I have felt assured in my faith that my father will be with me, always.

———

Those years served as a potent reminder of how quickly time moves. Each of those we lost had lived a full, beautiful life. Which, for me, made it easier to be at peace with their passing. But at the time the yearly succession of deaths felt relentless. We were losing the generation that had raised us. Processing that loss brought together those of us who had loved and been loved by Uncle Sherman, Aunt Mary, Shyamala, and my dad. Emotionally supporting each other through that realization—whether it was me helping her clear out Aunt Mary's home or her calling me every day as I was beginning to grieve for my daddy—fortified my friendship with Kamala. That support continues whenever we get the opportunity to remember. It is yet another gift of lifelong friends: they help us revive the lessons and legacy of the formative souls who are no longer with us.

Presence

Showing Up

We've all heard the adage "The only constant in life is change." I understand the hard truth and wisdom in that, but there's been another constant in my life, one I count on with as much certainty as I do the passing of time. It's been present through every swell of unfathomable tragedy and joy, through changes monumental and minute. That constant, collectively, is my best girlfriends. I trust that no matter how long it's been, or what has occurred in the interim, we are there to bolster one another and interact as we have through decades of change.

True friendship offers me a similar solace to my spirituality. It restores me, lifts me up, and is always there to remind me that I'm not alone in this world. Friendship has been essential in my life, in ways seemingly insignificant and also on those days when a phone call from a beloved friend has been the only thing to compel me to turn off *Law & Order*, put on a dress, get out of the house, and meet up at a new spot for a glass of wine.

There's a reason we stay connected to some people while others fall away. Each of my friends has a unique quality that I admire and continue to learn from as we age together. But the ones who have endured in my life are the friends who always find a way to be present, no matter what it takes.

———

Throughout Kamala's career, I was as present as possible for every campaign—and there were a lot of them. I did phone banks, fundraisers, canvassing—essentially, whatever I could manage in the time I had. Especially for the early races or the close ones, it was important to me that I demonstrate my support of her, and I always wanted her to know I was present.

December 2003 was the first of these major, landmark campaigns, when Kamala was making her run for district attorney of San Francisco. It was election day, and I had to be in Fresno for work, with meetings until 4:00 p.m. She'd be speaking at her headquarters back in the city at seven o'clock. The drive is about three hours, so as long as there wasn't any unexpected traffic, I'd be able to make it.

I'd assured her I would be there, so the moment I wrapped up with my last customer, I drove to San Francisco, stopping only to gas up—and even then I took care of it in a hurry. Nothing could have stopped me from making it to her event. I would have driven the wheels right off the rental car. I arrived at her headquarters at 3801 Third Street just as she was walking up to the podium. Catching sight of Shyamala and Aunt Mary standing in the large crowd, right up near the front, I nudged and shouldered my way through to stand near them as she delivered her victory speech for an election that she initially had not been favored to win.

I wanted her to know that I had made it, that I was there for her no matter what. In such situations (when she's in the zone and about to address the public), she'll often glance at me, notice, but stay focused. She always keeps her composure, but that glance signals to me that she has registered my presence while staying on point. I smiled as she gave me that knowing glance, then swiftly refocused as she got to the microphone.

The memory is particularly vivid in the catalog of Kamala's events, in part because I felt it was especially important for me to be there and in part because I've probably never driven with such reckless determination . . . but mostly because it was the first time I truly recognized the extent of the very significant strides she was making. It was the first of so many important speeches she would give in front of a large crowd that had just elected her (and for what it's worth, I'm confident that she is nowhere near done making such speeches).

To fully absorb the step she was taking felt like a very special, very thrilling moment. The crowd was fired up, and she was ready for it! She had successfully unseated a long-term incumbent (who also happened to be her former boss) who had been serving the city for a while. And of course, it was an exceptional accomplishment to step into the role of the city's first Black female DA.

The pride on the faces of Shyamala and Aunt Mary was perhaps the most extraordinary sight of the evening, especially as both women generally bore more stoic expressions. It was a beautiful triumph for everybody who had contributed to raising Kamala—especially those two women (unfortunately, Mrs. Shelton had passed away a few years prior)—and who had instilled in her the ethos of hard work, decency, and confidence. There was nothing she couldn't do.

The usual crew attended her official swearing in a month later, in early January 2004. It was extremely festive, serving as a lively tribute to the range of people who had supported Kamala throughout her run. It was held at the relatively small Herbst Theatre in San Francisco's Civic Center. Its capacity is under a thousand, and the room was absolutely packed. I feel confident saying that there's never been such voluminous, delighted cheering for a DA getting sworn in. Maya—who had also become a lawyer—was up onstage with her. Of course Shyamala was there as well, dressed in an elegant gray suit. I was overcome as I watched her holding a copy of the Bill of Rights, which Kamala laid her hand upon as she raised her head and proudly uttered the oath of office to the chief justice of the California Supreme Court.

Once it was done, the day turned festive in a way that, again, I simply can't imagine for most district attorneys. There were Asian dragon dancers, colorful banners waving in celebration, and every variety of person present to celebrate Kamala's first truly historic win—secured when neither of us was forty years old yet.

———

Seven years later, in January 2011, as she was getting sworn in as attorney general of the entire state of California, I thought back to that first win. So much had happened since that first campaign; it felt as if every year since had been a new era of my life. A similar crew, with some enormous absences, was gathered together for her swearing in at the California Museum for History, Women and the Arts, in Sacramento (California's capital).

Though of course it was a victory and a major milestone for Kamala, I knew how challenging it must be for her not to have Shyamala standing beside her. Nonetheless, there were

touches embedded in the ceremony that honored her presence, such as a Thillana performance by a classical Indian
dancer, Vidya Sundaram, and a Behag Ragam musical piece.

Aunt Mary, my mother, and I were there, along with the
Shelton daughters and the rest of Kamala's baseline crew
of supporters. Again there was a vibrant display of colors,
with the burned orange of the building itself serving as the
backdrop, complemented by bright state and city flags and
the flowy fuchsia and purple garments worn by the dancers. The diverse crowd seemed lit up from within as we
watched the proceedings.

Kamala—who never forgets where she came from or
who helped raise her—was very happy to let me know that
she had picked up Aunt Mary in Oakland and the two of
them had driven to the state capital together. Not only that;
Kamala had even arranged to have them stay in a hotel room
together. I can't imagine how honored Aunt Mary must have
felt to be given such a tribute, then to be able to witness
Kamala make history...again. As a further testament to the
women who had helped her from the start, she gave her oath
of office by laying her hand upon Mrs. Shelton's well-loved
Bible as the chief justice of California swore her in.

In her speech she took a long while to offer an explicit tribute to Shyamala, interestingly talking about how her mother
had chosen to break with the expectation that she would
return to India for her arranged marriage and had instead

made the choice to marry Kamala's father because of love. She stated that that was "one of the greatest expressions of optimism that any one of us makes. That choice made me. It made my sister Maya. And, for me, it has always summarized what it means to be Californian. Grabbing hold of your destiny, looking relentlessly forward, and having the courage to embrace change each and every day of your life."

I still have the campaign sign from that run, along with a picture we took in front of the podium after her rousing speech. I was so *proud*, because of everything she'd accomplished, but also because of how much of her had remained unchanged—because of the respect she had shown to Shyamala, to Aunt Mary, to Mrs. Shelton, to the Berkeley village and ethos, to all of us from her childhood whom she had invited to celebrate that moment. Each landmark celebration has been exciting to attend in its own way, and I've carried that feeling throughout all of them: I've just been so grateful, and so proud of my friend.

———

We scheduled one of our catch-up dinners for the week of my birthday in April 2012. I remember I brought her a little jacket that I had made for her, one of my little sewing creations. She was thrilled with it, or at least suggested as much! We were exchanging our usual chat, filling each other in on what was happening in our lives. But early in the meal, Kamala paused for a moment and smiled in a way I hadn't seen in a long time. It was as if we were teenagers!

"Wait. *What?*" I asked, eager to know what had made her expression change.

She told me about a man she had gone out with a few times, a lawyer of some sort from Southern California with whom she had been set up on a blind date. I could tell that there was something special about him. She just couldn't stop smiling as she told me a little more about Doug. I knew he must be quite a guy to have won her affection in such a fairly short time. As lifelong girlfriends, we had each kept regular tabs on anyone the other was dating seriously. I knew instinctively that this would not be the last I heard about him, and I hoped it wouldn't be long until I got to meet him.

Sure enough (and how time flies...), within two years Kamala called to share the wonderful news: they were getting married! I was so excited for her; my heart just swelled at the sound of pure happiness in her voice. As I had watched her continue to ascend professionally and politically, my one twinge of hope had been that she might find the right person to walk that path alongside her. We were in our late forties at the time, and she had finally found him.

I couldn't wait to find out all about the wedding plans and to learn what I could do to help. I knew it would be fabulous. Initially she talked about wanting to get married in Jamaica.

That sounded spectacular and added a nice, personal touch—of course she's half-Jamaican, and the vibe there is so relaxing. Plus, I thought it would be extra nice for Kamala to get away from the prying eyes of the US media. She knew I had traveled a great deal and would be ready to hop on a plane and go absolutely anywhere she proposed.

Though she's probably the busiest person I've ever met, she took it upon herself to coordinate everybody's schedules and to find a time and place that would be convenient for each of the relatively small handful of close guests they had invited. She called a few days later to check some dates with me and said that—considering the travel time for people from both coasts—she and Doug were thinking about Santa Barbara. I love Santa Barbara, loved the idea of a California wedding, and thought it sounded perfect: coastal, beautiful, and intimate.

The date was set for August 2014. Maya and her husband, Tony, hosted a family dinner the night before the wedding, which was when I finally had the chance to spend some time talking to Doug Emhoff and getting to know the man who had captured Kamala's heart. It was just a basic chat, with him asking me about my work, my children, and my long friendship with Kamala. He mostly observed and listened attentively, clearly displaying his genuine nature and his desire to learn more about the closest friends of his soon-to-be wife.

The weekend also gave me the opportunity to get to know

his children, Cole and Ella, each of them intelligent, gentle, and very kind. One can tell a lot about somebody by the relationship they share with their children. Both of Doug's kids project a similar warmth and generosity of spirit to their father—revealing as much through engaged conversation and sincere smiles. I knew that Kamala already cared for them deeply. She wanted them to be her family—and they seemed equally fond of her. From every angle this was a union that was meant to be, and the vibes were spectacular.

After the lovely dinner, back at the hotel, most of us stayed together in the lounge and enjoyed a nightcap. At one point Kamala started singing along to a Bob Marley song that was playing overhead. At the time, I was sitting next to Doug in the lounge. We were both watching Kamala sing, swaying from side to side, and with tears in my eyes, I told him—sincerely—that I had never seen her look so happy. She seemed so free, so comfortable, knowing that she was surrounded by her family, removed from any judgments or expectations. He smiled back at me with such genuine warmth. It was obvious to me (as it has become to the majority of the American public) that he has a beautiful heart, with eyes that reveal the deeply thoughtful, considerate human that he is. Turning back to watch her, he was beaming as much as she was; their adoration was as apparent as it was touching. That note of true love set the tone for a weekend of nonstop celebration.

The wedding ceremony was held at the Santa Barbara

County Courthouse, a National Historic Landmark with Spanish-style architecture that continues to serve as an active courthouse—making it a fitting match for Kamala: rich with history, beautiful, and still a place where justice is being delivered! The interior isn't what one might imagine when thinking of a court. It is filled with stunning murals, many of them bearing antique gold accents, which seemed coordinated with Kamala's elegant, champagne-colored dress. She looked positively stunning.

Maya was the officiant, adding yet another perfect touch to enhance the intimacy and family-themed ambiance of the whole wedding. As we stepped outside, there was a warm ocean breeze, with lush greenery all around us. It was simply gorgeous, all the more so because I knew that was exactly the atmosphere that Kamala and Doug wanted: elegant, private, and relaxing, the perfect scene in which to be married, surrounded by their closest friends and family.

———

The last election night party I went to (where Kamala was present) was on November 8, 2016, a date that makes a great number of people cringe. The evening started off on a high level of excitement, as all accounts suggested that Kamala would be winning her senatorial run by a landslide. That victory had essentially been assured ever since she had delivered an inspiring address at the 2012 Democratic National Convention, which had led to widespread encouragement for her to run for the upcoming California Senate seat that was being vacated by Barbara Boxer.

Presuming that she was going to win made it no less thrilling to watch the votes confirm that she would soon be heading to Washington as the second Black female senator and first South Asian senator. Her election party was held in downtown Los Angeles, at the Exchange LA nightclub.

Kamala and Doug had arranged to have a lovely family dinner beforehand, an opportunity for a small group of us to come together and celebrate as we watched the final votes come in for California and for the presidential race—both of which I think we all assumed were in the bag.

My son, Patrick, attended the family dinner with me and enjoyed being amid the excitement while he snapped candid pics of his auntie and me chatting. The dinner fulfilled its lovely purpose: it was an opportunity for Kamala to gather in an intimate setting with her closest family and friends before accepting her new position as a US senator. It was particularly special because, for the landmark occasion, members of Shyamala's immediate family had traveled all the way from India to support her. Other longtime de facto family members—me, Aubrey LaBrie, and others—had traveled from all over California. Even my mom had made the journey down and would be joining us a few hours later, after meeting up with my brother, to attend the more public official election party.

The night was one I'll never forget, though it was an extreme emotional roller coaster, with the energy by the end of the evening having plummeted to a very different plane from its triumphant beginning. While enjoying the family dinner, many of us were still taking the occasional peek on our mobile phones to catch up with the latest results for all the close races throughout the country, most notably the presidential race. There was also a muted TV overhead, which we were all checking from time to time. Though the California race had not yet officially been called, Kamala thanked us all for our support, and we cheered mightily and shed tears knowing that she was just on the verge of a historic Senate win, collectively marveling that after all her hard work and unceasing determination, she would soon be taking her place on the national stage.

I started noticing a few people looking panicked or just in shock, and a surreal, overwhelming uneasiness settled into the room. My son leaned toward me, whispering, "Mom. Trump might...win."

The possibility was too unreal to conceive of at that point. I shook off his terrifying suggestion and refocused my attention on making our way to the main hall of the Exchange to join the larger party. I wanted to find my mother and be sure that we were well placed to hear Kamala address the lively crowd that was waiting to hear her victory speech. Patrick and I separated from the group first in order to catch my mom and Ronny at the door and ensure they didn't have any difficulty getting in. The place was absolutely packed, literally wall-to-wall with supporters. Having located each other, the four of us went upstairs to the designated "family" section, where we had the ideal view of the stage. That also meant getting a perspective on the crowd below, many of whom were checking phones anxiously and starting to look frantic and confused.

Urgently trying to keep my focus on Kamala, I turned to my mom, and we spoke about how touching it was to see Kamala's aunts up onstage with her wearing their vibrant saris, and how very much this night would have meant to Shyamala.

I trust it would have been especially poignant for her to hear Kamala speak about the need to take action and take up the fight for justice. With Doug proudly by her side, she spoke about the need to fight for our ideals and rise to the occasion. She alluded to Coretta Scott King, by asserting, "The fight for civil rights, the fight for justice, the fight for equality must be fought and won with each generation."

The tenor of her words suggested she was preparing herself, and preparing all of us, for a very new, very unexpected kind of battle. Which, of course, she was.

Once the party had ended, Patrick decided to stay a while longer to hang with some of the people his age who had attended the family dinner. That left me alone in my car, forcing myself to listen to the shocking results of the presidential election, trying to digest it. I wound up driving home to Arcadia in tears, banging my hand against the steering wheel, just in total disbelief.

How could this have happened? Who were we? To me it felt like the end of the world.

The only small measure of comfort that I kept going back to was my knowledge that Kamala does not tolerate bullies. My knowledge that there was nobody better to be sending to Washington. My knowledge that she intended to fight for justice. As much as possible, she would play a role—a crucial role—in making sure he was never reelected.

I played back the words she had just spoken on the stage. Impassioned and completely self-possessed, she had told the crowded room, "Do not despair, do not be overwhelmed, do not throw up our hands when it is time to roll up our sleeves and fight for who we are."

———

The following year, though she was quickly becoming a nationally recognized and respected senator, Kamala still found loving ways to also show up for me and to remind me that we're family.

It was the summer of 2017, and I was at an on-site meeting

in Denver when Kamala called. After a bit of chatting, she told me that she wanted to see Patrick perform. I had been telling her about his acting for years, but her schedule had always been completely full, and she had never had the time or opportunity to see him onstage. Congress was about to go on recess, and she was going to be spending it at home (Los Angeles at the time).

"I want to go with you to see Patrick in Shakespeare in the Park," she said. She asked me for the dates and assured me she would find a way to attend.

Patrick is a company member with Independent Shakespeare Co. (ISC). The company is famous for its performances of the Shakespeare Set Free series, which attracts thousands of devoted, loyal fans from all over Southern California to Griffith Park during the summer. Friends, couples, and families (including pets) gather to picnic together under the stars and enjoy a spectacular presentation. Those in the know arrive early, before sunset, to scope out and claim a good spot as close to center stage as possible. Which means that as much as two hours before showtime, people start lining up their blankets and lawn chairs, making use of every inch of space in view of the stage.

For the summer of 2017, ISC was performing *Measure for Measure* and *The Two Gentlemen of Verona*. As promised, Kamala worked out her schedule, then called to confirm with me that she and Doug would be able to attend the final night's performance of *The Two Gentlemen of Verona*. It was bound to be a massive night for the company, with a packed house (or park). Needless to say, my son and I were both ecstatic that Kamala and Doug would be sharing this experience and new tradition with us. Patrick was especially excited about the fact that she would get to hear him sing. In addition to playing the role of Sir Eglamour, he was also one of the singers for the performance, which he loved—his voice is what got him into acting in the first place.

A few days in advance, Patrick told me that everything was confirmed with ISC and its security. It had taken care of the provisions and all precautions and was prepared for then-Senator Harris to attend. I remember Patrick asking me anxiously whether I felt sure that she would be there. I know Kamala. She doesn't dangle empty promises. She's a follow-through friend, and she does what she says she's going to do. And indeed, she made it work, which was a production in itself and entailed her staff being in close communication with ISC to ensure that all logistics were worked out. I was so excited to be with Kamala, but I also naturally became a little worried, considering she was a US senator with a rapidly rising profile (having very recently gone viral by proving her prosecutor's chops when grilling Jeff Sessions before his confirmation, to the point where he had responded to her efficient line of questioning by saying it was making him nervous) coming to hang on the lawn in a wide-open park.

I couldn't help but feel a little concerned for her safety. But I also knew that she doesn't let baseless fears get in her way, so I tried to stay positive.

To keep busy, I started prepping for the park early Saturday afternoon—packing up all kinds of cheese and grapes, wine, and plastic cups. Knowing all too well what it's like to linger out there on a hot summer's night, I ran out to buy a couple of mini fans that we could hang around our necks to keep us cool and deter bees and mosquitoes.

Usually I would plan to arrive by five o'clock to get a good parking and lawn spot, but my nerves and excitement were high, so I arrived closer to four. Marisa, ISC's communications director, approached me to let me know how excited and thankful the cast and crew were about Senator Harris attending. She showed me the path where her car would drive up and walked me over to the reserved VIP lawn chairs from which we would watch the show. When it was nearing the time for Kamala's car to arrive, I walked quickly over the grass to the edge of the path to greet her. Right on time, the sleek black SUV made its appearance as it slowly drove toward the stage. Out of nowhere, members of her security team dressed in plain clothes moved from the lawn toward the car. The driver got out and opened the rear passenger door for Kamala and Doug.

Kamala looked fabulous, but also comfortable and relaxed, dressed in white jeans, a loose top, and sneakers, her hair pulled back in a simple ponytail. As soon as she and I caught eyes, my shoulders relaxed, and we both started laughing as we approached each other. We embraced, squeezing each other tightly, then Doug gave me a big, warm hug. We all walked downhill on the grass toward the back of the stage, chatting with excitement. Marisa escorted us backstage and introduced Senator Harris to the artistic director and her husband, who's also the composer, both of them actors and owners of ISC. After obligatory introductions and greetings with cast members, Kamala turned to me and asked, "Where *is* he?" A few seconds later, Patrick came hustling from his dressing room trailer. Kamala saw him, smiled broadly, and opened her arms. "There he is!" she shouted exuberantly.

They caught up for a minute, and he let her know how much it meant to him that she was there. At one point the stage manager, Jenny, started talking with Kamala. She had freaked out when she saw her talking to Patrick. She'd grabbed David, another one of the actors (and an owner), and whispered, "She's here! Backstage!"

"Who?"

"Kamala Harris!"

David encouraged Jenny to go and talk to her, but she was too intimidated. She eventually went out as the whole crew was introduced, and David gently pushed her toward Kamala. The rest of the cast made room for her, and they started speaking. Jenny told Kamala how much she admired her, then spontaneously opened up about being a DACA (Deferred Action for Childhood Arrivals) child. A draft of Trump's executive order to terminate the DACA program had been leaked, provoking fear and panic for hundreds of thousands of "Dreamers." Jenny began crying as she asked Senator Harris to please help keep the DACA program. "I've lived here for most of my life, I went to school here, and I love being a part of this company…This is my home," she said, wiping away tears. It felt like an especially profound reveal, as it wasn't until then that several of her fellow cast members learned this about Jenny. Kamala hugged her, then pulled back but held on to her shoulders, looking Jenny directly in her eyes.

"I will fight for you. I will do everything I can do to make sure that that never happens. I have your back, Jenny, OK? You're going to be fine." Kamala gave her another comforting hug as most everybody watching the interaction started crying as well. Three years later, when the Supreme Court rejected the Trump administration's termination of the program, Jenny thought back to that night, surrounded by her theater family, when Senator Harris had told her that she was going to be OK.

The powerful moment was brought back to me again in January 2021, when Kamala—the child of two immigrants—got up and spoke about her and President Biden's upcoming immigration reform bill. I got choked up when she said they intended to grant green cards immediately to immigrants protected by DACA policies. She does what she says she's going to do.

Backstage, we all arranged ourselves for a group photo, then Senator Harris's name was announced, and she was escorted and introduced onstage. She offered the audience warm words about ISC, about free arts programs, and about how great it was to be back in her home state. "This is about showing the best of who LA is, the best of who California is, and what we can do better in our country."

The park erupted with cheers and she laughed, then concluded by stating that the festival brought "folks together around a common experience, especially in a world that right now is encouraging divisiveness. This is about showing that we are all in it together."

Waving to the crowd, who had gotten to their feet to give her a standing ovation, she was escorted through the crowd to join Doug and me in our lawn chairs. We settled right in comfortably. She never needs to take time to code-switch from politician to friend. She's always just Kamala. The two of them had also come prepared with a picnic basket of boxed dinners: chicken, salmon, and steak. She said she wasn't sure which I'd prefer, so they'd brought one of each.

The night was magical. We ate, whispered to each other throughout the show, and giggled like old times. During intermission and when the show was over, she graciously took selfies with all the audience members who had gathered around to capture a memory of her presence. Doug waited patiently, chatting with assorted people, smiling comfortably. In sum, it was an unforgettable night—for me, for Patrick, and for the ISC "family" and fans.

———

Kamala's profile continued to rise, boosted by her searing questioning of Brett Kavanaugh and widespread discussions about her potential as a presidential hopeful. I continued to always make sure that I showed up for her at milestone events. In January 2019 I attended the release party at the Wilshire Ebell Theatre in Los Angeles for Kamala's books: her memoir, *The Truths We Hold: An American Journey*; and her children's book, *Superheroes Are Everywhere*.

Beforehand, I met up with our friend Debby Dubose, so we could attend together. Debby and I had met a few years earlier, shortly after I relocated from the Bay Area to Southern California. A few months into our friendship, we figured out that we both knew Kamala. Debby is originally from Montreal, where she and her sister, April, attended high school with Maya and Kamala. Out of the millions of people in the Los Angeles area, she is the one person I had really become close with—which still strikes me as a remarkable coincidence.

Debby and I purchased our books, then hustled as close to

the stage as possible before the live interview with Kamala began. At the conclusion of her discussion and public signing, there was an opportunity for close friends and VIPs to personally greet her backstage, in a small room. Debby and I went back but kept to the side and waited for the crowd to dissipate. Finally everyone had cleared out, leaving just Kamala, Debby, and me in the dressing room, plus a security guard at the door. Kamala was thrilled to see Debby after all those years, as they hadn't reconnected since high school in Montreal.

"How is April?!" Kamala asked. April had been one of her best friends in Montreal (just as Debby had been for Maya). Debby showed us a few pics from her phone and caught her up on her sister. We told her how Debby and I had been connected by my only other friend in SoCal, Anthony. He had known she and I would hit it off, and he was right: she became my running buddy and good friend in LA.

Eventually I placed my stack of books on the table beside her: four of *The Truths We Hold* and two of *Superheroes Are Everywhere*. Without hesitation Kamala said, "Tell me what you need me to do, honey." As I handed each book to her and said the name of the recipient (my mom, Carole, Lauren, and my granddaughter Savannah, plus one of each book for me), she asked how they were doing, and we chatted a bit about each person. She took her time, being thoughtful about what special note she wanted to impart with each inscription. She passed the books back to me, then let us know she had to get going. We hugged for a long time, the same way we would as kids when she'd be leaving to return to Montreal, or later, when we'd both be heading back to college. She embraced Debby in the same way, with such heart that Debby let out a long "Ahhhh" that made the three of us laugh.

I waited until I got home before opening the books. I started with her children's book, smiling as I read about the superheroes in her life—starting, of course, with Shyamala, then going on to Maya and the rest of her family. I turned the page and sat up with tears filling my eyes as I read, "Heroes are best friends. My best friends and I cared about each other. When I was in kindergarten, I told a boy to stop teasing one of my best friends, and another time that best friend helped me when I fell on the playground. We all wanted to feel safe at school. My best friends were superheroes because they made one another feel safe."

The book references Mrs. Shelton's kindness, playing chess with Uncle Sherman, and reading with Aunt Mary. There are several other "superheroes" mentioned, as Kamala has been influenced and guided by all kinds of mentors who believed in her. In no way is her character tied exclusively to our village in Berkeley. But there was something un-deniably special, and safe, about our childhood and those who touched our early lives, helping us discover ourselves and the world around us.

I finished her children's book, delighted by the thought of reading it to my granddaughter. I put the rest of the books to the side and picked up my personal copy of her memoir. I smiled back at her on the cover and opened it to read her inscription to me: *Darling dearest best friend for life, from the beginning. I love you and thank you for sharing this journey with me. Love you!*

Determination

The First, but Not the Last

One week later, on Martin Luther King Jr. Day, January 21, 2019, Kamala officially announced that she would be running for president of the United States. Within the same week she held a massive rally in Oakland, attended by some twenty thousand people, to get her sizable local fan base fired up and ready for the wild journey ahead.

Never one to hold back a nod to her ancestors and all the extraordinary characters from Berkeley and Oakland who had helped raise her, she took to the mic at that rally and talked about how, "growing up in the East Bay, we were raised by a community with a deep belief in the promise of our country...a community where we were taught to see a world beyond ourselves, to be conscious and compassionate about the struggles of all people."

As a member of that community and as her friend for life, I fully supported her and told her I would be willing to do anything at all she needed to help with the campaign. She already had an impressive staff assembled, but I did what I could and followed the ups and downs of her run very closely. All her friends did. No matter what our occupations were, we (me, Carole, Kamala's dear friends Chrisette and Debbie Mesloh, the Sheltons, all the folks from home, my mom) came together, discussed how we could be most useful, and pooled our strengths to do whatever we could—big or small—to help with her campaign. Kamala and I texted each other fairly regularly as she crisscrossed the country for months on end.

In the fall of 2019, I cohosted a fundraiser in Oakland to help keep the momentum going for her campaign. Everything was all set, but then a week and a half before the big night, I had a terrible bike accident. It was September 17, the fundraiser was happening on Sunday the twenty-ninth, and I was a physical wreck: badly bruised all along my right side, with a chipped bone in my right elbow and a hideous busted bottom lip. I had been planning to make the five-hour-plus drive from Arcadia up to Oakland, but unexpectedly was going to have to do as much with a cast on my right arm. The timing was terrible.

Never one to bail out or make excuses, I pressed on. "I often drive with one hand anyway," I told myself. "I got this." But...hold up...how was I going to do my hair?! In little moments like these, "sister" friends come through. I called my dear friend Kim, whom I've known since second grade and who's been like a big sister to me. She readily agreed to meet me in my hotel room and do my hair Sunday morning. Aside from my hairstylist of nearly twenty years, Kim's probably the only person I would trust to do my hair. We caught up on some of the Bay Area goings-on while I did my best to simultaneously apply makeup with the use of only my right index and middle fingers.

The fundraiser was held at Eve's Waterfront in Jack London Square. Eve's sits on the water and is now an upscale seafood restaurant, but the venue has been reopened a couple of times under different ownership over the years. Back in the eighties and nineties, it was called the Rusty Scupper, and I had a lot of fun partying there back in the day. I forgot about my injuries as I mingled with the large crowd, catching up with people I hadn't seen in years. We reminisced about the old establishment and being there when we were younger. There was a built-in nostalgia to the place itself, and the whole event carried that kind of familiar atmosphere and energy. So many old friends came out to support Kamala. Carole was also a cohost, and members of the Shelton family showed up. My mom was there, of course, and had brought along several of her friends.

A few minutes before Kamala was going to address the crowd, she and Carole were tucked away to the side, out of sight. Kamala called out to me and beckoned me over for a quick hug and to tell me a funny memory they had been sharing, something about Carole's sister. As soon as she saw me in the light she stepped back and took a good look at me. "Stacey!! Honey, what *happened* to you?!"

I let out a big laugh and shook my head. "Bike accident. Long story, but I'm fine."

"Oh, honey. You sure?"

I smiled to reassure her. "I was avoiding being hit by a car and ended up crashing on the sidewalk. It was awful, but I'm OK!" She was about to get up and speak, but I intuited from her loving smile and gentler hug that she had registered the effort I had made, busted lip and all. Carole and I watched together as she was introduced and walked out in plain view, making a point of waving at the Sheltons and others we had known for most of our lives.

Kamala seemed so happy to see us and to be in her hometown, among people she loved and trusted. She didn't have her guard up in the same way she might have on the road. There was a positive, comfortable feeling in the room, with people of all ages enjoying the event. It wasn't a huge crowd, so it felt more intimate and low-key. And everybody who was there didn't only want to see her as our next president; we wanted to show her our love, support, and friendship!

At this point she'd been campaigning throughout the country for about ten months, shuttling around on her bus, interfacing with countless strangers, being interviewed and scrutinized, and having to keep up her game—all while living out of her suitcase, in hotels all over America. On top of that, she was still casting votes and listening to constituents and taking on bullies and fulfilling her duties as a senator on high-profile committees. I can't imagine that level of stress, exhaustion, exposure, and 24-7 publicity. For this weekend at least, she was back with people she could trust and relax around. You could tell what a relief it was. She carried herself with palpable comfort and ease, laughing with her oldest friends in that reminiscent atmosphere.

When she stepped up to the mic, there was an eruption of welcoming hometown cheers. After her rousing speech of gratitude, stoking excitement and hope in the local crowd, friends and family lined up to take photos. My mom and I decided to wait our turn, so we stood near the end. When she saw me again she shook her head with a little laugh as she greeted Doris with a big embrace.

For our photograph we maneuvered ourselves to conceal my cast behind her, smiling broadly and almost mischievously, as if only the two of us were in on a secret. The picture is one of my favorite photos of all time. It doesn't only remind me of how my dear friend campaigned to become president of the United States. For me it symbolizes resilience, endurance, and the ability for friends to find joy, even in very uncomfortable circumstances! It just makes me so proud every time I look at it.

The following month I was on a business trip in Cleveland, Ohio, seeing several of my clients and their teams. These meetings happened to take place the same week that one of the Democratic presidential debates (hosted by CNN and the *New York Times*) was being held in Westerville, Ohio, at Otterbein University.

Though it would be a squeeze, I knew I had to get there if at all possible. It was Kamala. In a presidential debate! I'd find a way. I figured out the distance between where I was staying and where the debate was going to be held, calculated that I could reasonably drive there and back in time to make all my meetings, and reached out to Maya to see if I could attend. Always efficient, she generously looked into it quickly and got back to me, confirming that I would have a ticket and that she'd send me all the logistics.

I hit the road to Otterbein as soon as my meetings ended. It was only about a two-hour drive, enough time for me to really marvel at the fact that I was about to see Kamala fighting to be the leader of our nation. I remembered all the pillars of our shared past and imagined how proud each of them would be to see her up on the stage.

Once I arrived at the university, I waited—eager but patient—in the long line to get in. Finally the ushers pointed the way to my seat: I had a great vantage point, where I'd be able to see all the candidates! Doug and Meena walked in shortly after I did; we exchanged quick hellos and big hugs as folks buzzed around to find their assigned seats.

I got goose bumps when I saw Kamala walking out on the stage. In her first response to the panel of moderators, she spoke about being observant and paying attention, paraphrasing Maya Angelou to drive home her point: "Listen to somebody when they tell you who they are the first time." She pulled absolutely no punches in quickly asserting that Donald Trump was the most corrupt and unpatriotic president we had ever had. It was impossible not to think of Shyamala with that opening. Profound, artful, impassioned, and fearless—all qualities I associate with Kamala's mom.

Shortly after, she brought it back to herself, responding to a question about taxes by talking about Shyamala working so hard to raise her and Maya, coming home late at night, cooking dinner, and (after the girls had gone to bed) sitting up at their kitchen table, trying to make it work for their family. I could picture that kitchen table. As a kid I had never considered what exactly it would have meant for Shyamala, with the help of our community, to raise her daughters. But as a mother who has spent more than a few nights up late, trying to figure out how on earth I was going to get my two children through college, I was filled with fresh awe over Shyamala's struggle and success.

Throughout the increasingly heated debate, Kamala often

looked deep in thought during questions, a trait of hers I'd always noticed. She's always listening...but she's also thinking ahead. I flashed back to her previous campaign rallies I had attended and tried to imagine the enormous amount of preparation she must have done for tonight as she stood among eleven others during the final stages of one of our overcrowded presidential primaries. I was frustrated that she didn't get more time to speak, but I was so proud every time she managed to get a word in. She held her own, spoke her truth, and never faltered. What made it all the more impressive to me was that I knew it really was her truth and that she believed intensely in everything she was saying. She sounded like herself, not like some canned politician who was just saying the right thing for the audience.

Toward the end of the evening, Kamala brought up her mother's legacy one last time, telling an abbreviated version of the story of Shyamala leaving India alone, arriving in California, getting involved in the Civil Rights Movement, marrying, and having her and Maya. I couldn't help but tear up when she turned to the crowd directly, stating, "My mother convinced us that we could do anything." She finished by insisting that she was running for president to make sure that the American dream—embodied by Shyamala—held true. A familiar rush of pride overwhelmed me; I could barely contain myself!

After the debate ended, the attendees started moving

toward the exits. I remained standing near my seat, savoring the moment, thrilled that I had been able to be present for another step on her historic path. Kamala and some of the other candidates remained onstage, chatting with admirers and media who had moved closer. I started making my way to the stage in hopes of making eye contact with her, if only for a quick glance. The crowd grew tighter the closer I got, but when I thought I was close enough for her to hear me, I called out her name, just once. She popped her head up alertly and started looking around: she had heard me! I waved frantically until our eyes finally locked.

"That's my best friend!" she shouted.

The crowd considerately parted and stepped aside enough to form a tiny path so I could make my way to the stage. As soon as I was in reach we grasped each other's hands. I could feel our powerful bond coursing between us. We were both smiling so broadly, I felt my heart was going to burst. She asked me to come backstage with her, but it was late and I had to make it through the debate traffic and then on to the two-hour drive back to Cleveland. She knew I'd shown up, and that—as ever—I'd be there to support her.

———

Throughout her presidential campaign, Kamala proved her mettle, and her resilience was put to the test. She was accustomed to winning and had put so much of herself into the fight. Knowing Kamala and how determined she is, I knew she would keep her sights and spirits high. She was careful to neither confirm nor deny she was being considered for the vice-presidential ticket or any other position in the cabinet should the Democrats pull off the win.

Kamala being discreet about her goals didn't stop Carole and me or my mom and me from speculating about the exciting possibilities! Such chatter and discussion among friends ramped up once Biden had secured the nomination—in large part thanks to the votes of Black Democrats. When he announced that he would be choosing a woman for his running mate, I couldn't help but hope. The media started discussing the likelihood that Kamala would be on his list. I had to believe that there was another play, as I still felt so strongly that there was no better choice for the country.

And indeed, after an extensive, grueling process, she earned her way onto the ticket—a decision I got wind of on Tuesday, August 11. I was in the middle of a work conference call (which has basically been my life during the pandemic— just Monday-through-Friday, all-day conference calls). So I was on my computer, and all of a sudden my personal phone started absolutely blowing up, *buzz buzz buzz*: text messages, phone calls—they just didn't stop. Unfortunately I was speaking during this meeting, however, so I was unable to check who it was or unlock my phone to see what was going on.

I knew Biden's decision was imminent, and that Kamala was among the last four candidates he was considering seriously. I also knew that I would be getting a whole lot of messages whether he had chosen her or one of the other three women. Either way, I was desperate to finish my call and see which way it had gone. My work phone suddenly started doing the same thing: alerting me to strings of texts and attempted calls.

Finally I finished speaking, but I still had to remain on the call. I couldn't wait any longer. I went ahead and checked my phone. The first text I saw was from Carole. The exclamation points and emojis alone made it clear that Kamala had been chosen.

––––––––

Three months later, after a fall filled with efforts for the Biden/Harris campaign, the big day arrived. Like most engaged Americans, my friends and family were absolutely glued to the presidential race from the moment news outlets started announcing states. My heart raced anxiously that first night, as the map of the country seemed to be filling up with states that had gone red. My phone didn't stop buzzing as text messages were exchanged in a steady stream pretty much around the clock. We were all just so anxious. The majority of my consistent exchanges were with Carole, and of course my mom.

Carole Porter had played a major role in Kamala's presidential campaign in the Bay Area, then immediately switched gears to support the Biden/Harris ticket in every way possible. My mom had been closely tracking Kamala's potential rise at every key moment—not just during her presidential run, but through all the key moments of her tenure as senator and every campaign before that. She had been so enthusiastic about Kamala being Biden's VP pick, and—based on my phone—appeared to stay up through the night for several days, texting our family group nonstop as the results dragged on for what some people have referred to as the longest Tuesday of our lives!

At what felt like dawn on November 6, I got a text from Carole: **45 needs GA to win…GA is blue!** Almost immediately afterward she sent a message that still gives me chills: **We have a first woman VP from West Berkeley/Oakland! BLACK WOMEN delivered Joe to nomination & BLACK WOMEN (Stacey Abrams) delivered GA for the win!!**

We would all see the work of Stacey Abrams confirmed once again in the recount for Georgia, which yielded Democratic victory and control of the Senate. But the race wasn't called until the morning of November 7, when Pennsylvania delivered enough electoral votes to push Biden over the requisite threshold of 270.

Around the same time, my mom sent a moving message to our family group: **They called it! My white neighbors are out** shouting and dancing in the street. I'm cheering with them from the kitchen window! YES! Kamala is VP! Oh wow! Now I'm crying again. This is beautiful. Now my children and my children's children's lives will be saved. I was donating, reminding people to vote. I was thinking of all of you. I smiled through tears, imagining my mom cheering out the window, full of feisty, celebratory passion. She had been involved for the whole run, always active, fighting to make this happen. I thought of how thrilled my father would have been—for Kamala, for Berkeley, and for the country. I imagined Uncle Sherman coming by the house with a big smile on his face, briskly entering and hustling through to celebrate with Daddy, and maybe to sit down with him to have a chat about how it had all gone down.

Carole forwarded a clip of a parade that was being held in Oakland. People had taken to the streets and were dancing and cheering, as if some sort of spell had been broken. It was so moving to see real joy on those streets again and to witness—on everyone's face—such bright, genuine expressions of relief, hope, and celebration. It was all the more special to watch that energy and activity take place where we had grown up, where it had all begun. They were rejoicing in our old stomping grounds. There were people celebrating in Jack London Square and that part of Oakland where my mom and Shyamala took me, Ronny, Kamala, and Maya to the Kwanzaa festival. The parade passed by Children's Fairyland and the Grand Lake Theatre, within sight of our condominium building by the lake, where Kamala and I had started carving out our own paths and hosted the Mother's Day brunch. As I watched the clip, the past and present merged in my mind. This was our home, our roots. It was a glimpse into who we were, where we had come from, and how we had been raised. At the same time, it was a vision of our new reality and of the future as Biden/Harris signs were waved and renewed hope surged through those familiar streets.

With the projection guaranteed, I texted Maya, **It's a wrap! Biden is #46!!! Your sister, my dear friend, is the first woman and Black female VP of the USA!!! Tears of joy!**

Finally I texted Kamala, knowing I would never be able to put my sense of elation into words. **You did it!!!!! You'll be in the history books my dear friend!** I added an abundance of crying emojis and blue hearts, knowing I didn't need to use words; she would be well aware of how I felt.

In the midst of the ineffable exhilaration I was experiencing, media requests started pouring in for Carole and me from ABC, Fox 11 Los Angeles, CNN, MSNBC. People with a close connection to her, who were allowed to speak freely, were in high demand for commentary. I agreed without reservation (though I was always incredibly nervous) because I knew I had nothing but the deepest and most genuine sentiments of praise to offer our Madam Vice President elect!

I gave a few interviews, but I was still able to tune in to watch Kamala greet an exuberant nation and introduce President-elect Biden for the first time for his acceptance speech from Wilmington, Delaware. It was held at a massive open lot filled with honking cars and all kinds of Americans who could finally hope again, waving their flags high in the air.

When Kamala walked out onto the platform, dressed in a beautiful white suit—honoring the suffragettes who had cleared the way—my heart was full. I thought of the past four years and everything the country had endured, of the horrors we had seen: white supremacy endorsed, children stripped from their parents, the needs of our beautiful planet cast aside, endless lies, all the pent-up misery, culminating in the devastating trauma of the pandemic.

Nobody can reverse the damage done. Nobody can erase those difficult, divided years. But the sight of her taking the stage signaled a new dawn. Her speech, delivered with a voice and face that were so familiar and so genuine to me, made me feel I was awakening from a nightmare, or finally coming up for air.

The fact that it was Kamala, the same Kamala that she has always been, made it all the more reassuring. Because I could trust what I saw. Because I could believe what I heard. Because when she says she's going to do something, she delivers. I watched through tears as the camera flashed to young girls looking up at her with hope and women my mom's age sobbing with relief. I waited, knowing that—just as she always has—she would find a way to pay tribute to Shyamala:

When she came here from India at the age of nineteen, she maybe didn't quite imagine this moment. But she believed so deeply in an America where a moment like this is possible. And so, I'm thinking about her and about the generations of women—Black women, Asian, white, Latina, Native American women who throughout our nation's history have paved the way for this moment tonight. Women who fought and sacrificed so much for equality, and liberty, and justice for all, including the Black women who are often, too often overlooked, but so often prove that they are the backbone of our democracy.... Tonight I reflect on their struggle, their determination, and the strength of their vision—to see what can be, unburdened by what has been. And I stand on their shoulders. And what a testament it is to Joe's character that he had the audacity to break one of the most substantial barriers that exists in our country and select a woman as his vice president.

Overcome, I picked up my phone and called my mom.
"This has been a happy day, love," she said.
"It sure has."

"We can look forward to a positive, better country now. This was divine intervention, to get us out of this pain and chaos. And they complement each other—Kamala and Biden. I cried again."

"I did too."

"I just wish Shyamala and your dad were here to see this."

"I do too, Mom. I do too."

The following week, once everything had settled down a little bit, Kamala and I had our first real conversation on November 14, when I was in Orlando for my nephew's SpaceX launch. It would be the last day that I would be able to reach her through her personal mobile phone. She made a point of telling me to take COVID very seriously and take care of myself. I assured her I was doing just that and always wore two masks. Before hanging up (and this is frequently how we've ended conversations), we both acknowledged that we would be there for each other, in it together, until the end.

———————

Two and a half months later, I was standing amid Kamala's family at the Lincoln Memorial Reflecting Pool, waiting for her to give her inaugural vice-presidential address. The vibrant colors and that sense of renewed hope that had been inspired by the inauguration remained within me, filling me with comfort. The feeling in the air was curiously familiar.

I knew that feeling, that mingling of vibrant optimism and the anticipation of work to be done, but done for good reason. It was the blend of energies I associate with my child-hood and with growing up in Berkeley. That feeling was only reinforced as I looked down the row at the Shelton daughters, their faces bright. Through their eyes I saw Mrs. Shelton, the matriarch of our community, and felt the love and warmth of her presence.

Basking in a feeling I can only describe as being home, I closed my eyes and envisioned Uncle Sherman and Aunt Mary, in all their wisdom, smiling down, perhaps alongside my dad, offering up the occasional "Right on!" My mom was apparently thinking the same thing. She texted the family: **I'm so happy and so proud of Kamala. I wish her mother, Mary, Sherman, and your dad were here to witness this. I know their spirits are with her. Like a breath of fresh air.**

Watching Kamala approach the podium to address the nation and the world, I flashed back to where she had started her journey and to the will and resilience it had required for her to continue climbing. I don't presume to know the world of politics inside out, or the ways of Washington, but I do know that—especially for a woman of color—these climbs don't have a summit, or at least not one where you can take it easy. She will have to prove herself consistently, time and time again. That made me consider both my mom and Shyamala, when they were starting out in their fields, then into their thirties with children, their forties, and our age now. In different fields but with similar tools, they achieved great heights, encouraging independence and courage throughout. I wish this weren't the case, but the lesson my grandparents passed down to my mom and my mom passed down to me—"You're going to have to work twice as hard as anybody else"—still rings true today, decades on. That would be a daunting, profoundly frustrating prospect for most people; but it hasn't been for Kamala, nor will it be.

Having shared many of her early influences, I felt nothing but respect and gratitude for Kamala's steadfast commitment to honoring the legacies of our earliest days. Yet even as I recognize these roots and their consistency, I know that at the end of any day or any journey, no matter the office, no matter how far she has ascended, Kamala has always just been herself with me. In that moment beside the Reflecting Pool, as throughout all the moments I've spent looking back on how we got there, I was left with a smile, knowing I was truly blessed to have such a wonderful friend in my life. A friend under any circumstances. Until the end.

Acknowledgments

Domenica Alioto—your intuition and insight is amazing. You see inside people and seek to understand them. You are such a brilliant writer; thank you for educating me along the way as we collaborated on my book. Working with you was an experience I will always cherish.

My family—my amazing daughter, Lauren, cherished granddaughters Savannah and Callie, and my son-in-law, Shawn, we live on through our children and their children (it's what gives life meaning); thank you for these two blessed gifts. My brother, Ronny, thank you for sharing your perspective and lessons learned from Uncle Sherman. Like our father, you can deliver a powerful message with only a few words. My sister-in-law, Dina, thank you for your support and encouragement during my many endeavors. Niece Mia and nephew Ronny Jr., Auntie is so proud of you; you are following in your parents' footsteps of displaying passion, purpose, and grace.

My Batiste family—your endless support and love over the decades means more to me than you will ever know.

Patrick Jr., my son and my "ride or die"—you have been my sounding board throughout this process. Thank you for your sharp wit, humor, and kind heart. We made it through 2020 together focusing on what matters most—our dreams, health, friends, and family.

Sean Desmond—thank you for believing in me. You remained engaged and provided great insight throughout the entire book writing process.

David Doerrer—many thanks for trusting in a newbie and agreeing to represent me. I appreciate your guidance and support along the way.

S. B. Kleinman—thank you for picking up on the little things that made such a difference. Your copyediting was spot on.

The Twelve team—Rachel Kambury, Megan Perritt-Jacobson, Estefania Acquaviva, Alisa Garza, Mari C. Okuda, Michael Gaudet, and Jennifer Tordy, thanks for being "all in" with me. You were an awesome team to work with, well-organized and efficient.

Jarrod Taylor—special thanks for listening to my vision for the cover, enhancing it, and bringing it to life in such a lovely way.

Harvey Livingston—you have been my boss at least three times over the decades. Thank you for also being my mentor and friend. Your habit of "always teaching" has a great impact on people. You truly want the very best for your folks and you bring out the very best in us.

Michael Howard—thank you for your behind-the-scenes fact-checking and independent research. You made sure we got it right!

Cherished best friends—Crystal, Colette, Michelle, and Kim, I don't know where I'd be without your unconditional love. Our sisterhood means everything to me.

My sister-friend Cyndi—thank you for always being there for me. Somehow you always know when to call or text and almost always with a crazy, funny story to share with me. I learn so much from you and love you dearly.

Carole Porter—our paths have crossed several times since becoming friends in the fifth grade, when our kids attended Shelton's together, and most recently while supporting Kamala's presidential campaign. Thank you for always providing sound advice and for trusting me with your words. I'm looking forward to what's next for us along our journey.

Oscar Jackson Jr., aka Paris—my "brother," you planted the seed and encouraged me to start writing. Thank you for bringing together the necessary resources to make this book

ACKNOWLEDGMENTS

possible. Thank you for truly *seeing me* and wanting nothing but the best for me.

Madam Vice President Kamala Harris—you have inspired me my entire life; even when we were kids and teenagers I looked up to you. Thank you for sharing your incredible journey with me. I will never forget where we come from and the everyday people who overlapped in our lives, each one of whom made extraordinary impacts.

Doris Johnson—Mom, thank you for your sharp memory and the interesting way you have always told your life stories. You taught me how to be a devoted mother and also how to go after what I want in life. I get my drive, tenacity, and creativity from you. Thank you for being my *research assistant extraordinaire* and my forever Yell Leader, always in my corner!

About the Author

Stacey Johnson-Batiste has extensive experience leading sales teams that provide communication services to business customers across the nation. She is currently a national sales channel manager within AT&T's Alliance Channel, where she manages third-party firms that sell products and services on behalf of AT&T. Responsibilities include operational leadership and growing strategic revenue. She was an honoree featured in *CRN* magazine's Power 100: The Most Powerful Women of the Channel 2018.

Stacey received her bachelor of science degree in organizational behavior from the University of San Francisco. She has completed years of leadership and development programs through AT&T University. Stacey is a certified professional training instructor, a graduate of the Data Communications Institute, and a certified sales coach in addition to receiving data and telecommunication product-specific certifications.

Stacey is a loving mother to a daughter, son, and two granddaughters. She is passionate about the protection of animals and the preservation of wildlife. Her hobbies include designing and sewing clothes, golfing, gardening, and fitness. In addition to spending quality time with family, she cherishes time spent with her close girlfriends—she considers sisterhood a precious gift.